RUN YOUR MUSIC BUSINESS™

HOW TO LICENSE YOUR MUSIC, NEGOTIATE CONTRACTS, PAY BUSINESS TAXES & WORK FULL-TIME IN MUSIC

VOLUME 2, MUSIC LAW SERIES™

BY ATTORNEY AUDREY K. CHISHOLM

RUN YOUR MUSIC BUSINESS™

Copyright © 2014 by Audrey K. Chisholm, Esq.

www.RunYourMusicBusiness.com

Published by Greenlight Books & Publishing, LLC

www.GreenlightBooks.org

All rights reserved. Except as permitted under the United States Copyright Act of 1976, no part of this publication may be reproduced or distributed in any form or by any means, stored in a database or retrieval system, without the prior written permission of the publisher.

DISCLAIMER: This publication is designed to provide competent and reliable information regarding the subject matter covered. However, it is sold with the understanding that the author and publisher are not engaged in rendering legal, financial, tax or other professional advice. Laws and practices often vary from state to state and if legal or other expert assistance is required, the services of a professional should be sought. Similarly, some information may be out of date even upon publication. The author and publisher specifically disclaim any liability that is incurred from the use or application of the contents of this book. Every effort has been made to accurately represent the potential of the advice contained within this publication. However, the author cannot and does not guarantee any degree of success as a result of the following advice. As with any business endeavor, there is no express guarantee that you will achieve specific results.

DISCLAIMER: The professionals or companies referred in this book are not employees or agents of Audrey K. Chisholm or Chisholm Law Firm, LLC. It is entirely up to you to enter into a direct contract or otherwise reach agreement with a professional and we do not guarantee or warrant their performance or the outcome or quality of the services performed. Should you have a dispute with the professional, you must address such dispute with the professional directly. By accepting any referral referenced in this book, you hereby agree to release Audrey K. Chisholm, Chisholm Law Firm and its officers, agents, and employees from any damages or claims arising out of or in any way connected with disputes and your dealings with the professional.

Acknowledgements

I would like to thank God for loving me unconditionally and granting me this tremendous opportunity. To my loving husband, Dr. Juan P. Chisholm, I am eternally grateful for the privilege of being your wife.

Dedication

I dedicate this book to my daughter. You have brought indescribable joy to my life! May I live in such a way as to bless your life in the same remarkable way that you have blessed mine.

Giving Back

A portion of all proceeds from book sales will be donated to 501(c)(3) charitable non-profit organizations to support education and entrepreneurship.

Get the "5 Streams of Royalties Your Music Should Be Earning" Chart Free by Signing up for our Mailing List at:
www.RunYourMusicBusiness.com

Table of Contents

Acknowledgements 3
Dedication 3
Giving Back 3

Why You Should Read This Book 11

Chapter 1: Planning to Succeed 15

Chapter 2: Get Paid Licensing Your Music 19
   What is Music Licensing? 19
      Why Should You License Your Music? 19
   How to Build Your Own Music Catalog 20
      Build Your Music Catalog by Writing Music 20
      Build Your Music Catalog by Buying Music 21
   How to Collect Performance Royalties 22
      What are Performing Rights Societies? 23
      How do they Collect and Pay Performance Royalties? 23
      Can you license music yourself if you are affiliated with BMI or ASCAP? 24
      How to Register with a Performing Rights Society 24
      How to Setup Your Own Publishing Company 25
   How to Setup Licensing Deals 27
      How to Contact Potential Buyers 28
   Negotiating Licensing Deals Yourself 29
   Hire Professionals to "Shop" Your Music. 31
      How to find people to help you. 33

How to Earn Royalties from Compulsory Licenses 34
How to Collect Mechanical Royalties from Your Music 35

Chapter 3: Producer Agreements 37
What are Producer Agreements? 37
    Why You Need One? 37
    When should you mention the Producer Agreement? 38
    Standard Terms of Producer Agreements 39
    What are Key Terms you Should Negotiate? 42

Chapter 4: Songwriter Agreements 47
    Types of Songwriter Agreements 47
    What are Key Terms in Songwriter Agreements? 49
    What are Key Terms you Should Negotiate? 51

Chapter 5: Recording Artist Agreements 57
Why do Artists Sign with Record Labels? 57
    How Record Labels Add Value to Artists 58
    How to Know if Your Label Can Deliver 61
    What are the Disadvantages of Signing with a Label? 65
    How Do Signed Artists Make Money? 67
How Can Artists Protect Themselves 68
    How do Major Recording Artists End up Broke? 69
    Key Terms in Recording Artist Agreements 69
    Key Terms to Negotiate 76

Chapter 6: How to Work Full Time in Music 79
    Know How Much Money You Need 79

What is Money Management? 81

How to Manage Your Money 82

Track the Money You Make 83

Track the Money You Spend 85

Track Money People Owe You 86

Track the Money You Owe People 87

Track Your Inventory 88

Chapter 7: How to Know if Your Business is Growing 91

Music Business Numbers 92

Artist/Band/Musician Numbers 92

Songwriter/Producer Numbers 95

Record Label Numbers 97

Chapter 8: How to Know if Your Business is Profitable 101

What are Financial Statements 101

Why Financial Statements Are Important 102

4 Types of Financial Statements 103

    1.   Income Statement / Profit & Loss Statement (P&L) 104

    2.   Balance Sheet 104

    3.   Statement of Cash Flows 105

    4.   Statement of Owner's Equity 106

How to Create Financial Statements 107

Chapter 9: How to Achieve your Financial Goals 109

What is a Budget? 109

How Budgets Help Grow Your Business 109

How to Create a Budget 112

The Importance of Controlling Expenses. 114

Chapter 10: Managing Debt & Credit 117
Ways to Manage Debt Responsibly 117
10 Ways to Improve Your Credit Score 121

Chapter 11: How to Run your Business 125
How You Run Your Business Matters 125
10 Ways to Avoid IRS Trouble 126
How to Hold Business Meetings 129
Developing a Strategic Plan for your Business 133
5 Steps to a Powerful Plan of Action 134

Chapter 12: Business Recordkeeping 139
Financial Records 139
Business Records 142
Tax Records 143

Chapter 13: Filing Business Taxes 145
Taxes for Sole Proprietors 146
Taxes for Partnerships 147
Taxes for Limited Liability Companies (LLC) 149
Taxes for Corporations 150

Chapter 14: Building Your Team 153
Why You Need an Attorney 155
   How to afford an attorney 158
   What to look for in a good lawyer 159
   How to find a good lawyer 161

Why you need an Accountant 161
    How to find a good accountant 162

Chapter 15: Give Back 167
How Giving Back Benefits You..167
Ways to Give Back..170
Encourage Others to Give Back 174

Final Words from the Author 179

About the Author 181

Why You Should Read This Book

Maybe you've read my first book in the Music Law Series™, *Start Your Music Business*™, or maybe you haven't. Regardless, if you are serious about growing your music business as an artist, musician, songwriter, independent record label or producer, then this book is for you.

You know that you have the talent - and you are probably already doing things with your music. Yet, you realize that something is missing. You need to *know* more in order to take your music to the next level.

You need to know how to license your music to maximize your song related income. You need to know how to negotiate producer agreements, songwriter agreements, and recording artist agreements to make sure you're not being cheated. You may understand a little about music publishing from my first book, but want to know how to setup your own publishing company and grow your music catalog. You know that you need to pay business taxes, but you need a straightforward explanation as to which forms to complete to make sure you comply with the law.

Perhaps you have dreamed of working full-time for yourself but need to know how to strategically position the money that you make and how to make more of it to become financially independent in the music industry. Most importantly, you need answers to all of these questions in plain English with examples and easy to understand steps. If you agree with any of the things I've just said, then this book is for you.

My reason for writing this book is simple: I am passionate about empowering artists, songwriters, musicians and producers with the legal and business acumen they need in order to succeed in the 21st century music industry.

I am a successful full-time practicing attorney and owner of my own law firm. My background as a corporate attorney has allowed me to negotiate multi-million dollar deals, represent Fortune 500 companies and strategically advise my clients using business and legal principles in order to further their goals.

I began representing musicians, songwriters, artists, bands, record labels and producers in addition to my corporate clients. Many of them had incredible talent yet did not understand how to leverage business and legal principles in order to grow their music businesses. I found that they all had the same questions about business and law.

I began working with them as clients and helping them structure their music empires in order to help them achieve their goals. As a result, my clients include record labels, songwriters, producers and artists whose works have been featured on MTV®, American Idol®, VH1®, Oxygen Network®, NFL® commercials and more. I have negotiated major recording deals with companies such as Disney® and have spoken to audiences of over 13,000 people around the country.

I am passionate about empowering talented musicians, artists, songwriters and producers because I am a musician. I have performed all over the world, but chose to pursue my love for business and law instead of a career in music. As a result, I understand the advantages major record labels and industry executives have due to their access to strategic legal and business advice through lawyers such as myself. I believe that musicians, artists, songwriters and producers should have access to the same information. I enjoy bridging the gap by communicating complicated legal and business concepts in a simple and easy to understand manner.

This book will not teach you how to write a hit song or how to become a great artist. However, it will equip you with the business and legal information you need to know to legally run and grow your own successful music business in order to achieve your goals.

Feel free to e-mail me your questions, comments and thoughts throughout this journey at **Audrey@RunYourMusicBusiness.com**

Chapter 1: Planning to Succeed

Welcome to book two in the Music Law Series™ *"Run Your Music Business™."* In my first book, *"Start Your Music Business™"*, we talked about how to start your music business. We discussed the different types of businesses (LLCs, corporations, partnerships, etc.) and how to set them up properly and legally. We covered how to protect the name of your music business by applying for a federal trademark and listed the steps to complete the federal registration process. We talked about how to completely own your music and your "masters" and how to register your songs with the U.S. Copyright Office for maximum legal protection. We discussed the different types of copyrights and how to know which one you need. We also covered how to legally use other people's music through sampling and how to protect yourself when you co-write a song. We wrapped things up by introducing music publishing and how to earn royalties from your music. We explained the different types of royalties your music should be earning from record sales, movies, commercials, public performances, digital downloads, digital streaming and much more.

If you haven't read my first book, *"Start Your Music Business™"*, I highly recommend that you do because this book will assume that you at least understand those basic concepts in music and entertainment law and will build upon that foundation. To pick up a copy, please visit: www.StartYourMusicBusiness.com

Now that you understand the foundational principles and have started your music business, it's time to learn how to effectively run your music business. Why is this important? Sometimes we think that successful people were simply born with something that the rest of us were not. For example, we attribute their success to them having a better upbringing, a better education, more money or access to industry contacts and opportunities. Of course, all of these factors can play a role. However, I have found that the one universal characteristic that allows people without many of those "advantages" to still succeed, myself included, is to have a *plan* and stick with it.

What do I mean by a plan? Well, almost anyone can follow steps and start a music business. Many people start businesses all of the time. However, the difference between people in the music industry that are successful versus people that are not has to do with how they choose to *run* their music businesses.

Successful artists, producers, musicians, and songwriters *plan* for success. They have a *plan* for how they handle negotiating contracts. They have a *plan* for how they spend their money and they have a *plan* for what they choose to do with their time. They have a *plan* for reviewing their business operations and making sure that they are constantly growing and improving. Their ability to follow their plan day after day and year after year, instead of jumping ship every time things become difficult, helps them achieve.

This is what *Run Your Music Business*™ is all about. I have been fortunate to build several successful businesses, and work with artists, producers, songwriters, and musicians that have achieved their goals in the music industry. As a result, this book will give you a *plan* for successfully running your music business as a means of achieving your goals. Many of these principles can be universally applied to any business, but we're focusing specifically on music businesses.

In this book, we're going to start by explaining how to license your music to maximize your song related income. This will allow you to make money when other people use your songs. This means learning how to properly set-up your own publishing company and how to strategically grow your music catalog.

We will then discuss how to negotiate producer agreements, songwriter agreements, and recording artist agreements to make sure you're not being cheated and that you get the best terms possible. Once we've covered contracts, we will discuss how to work full-time in music for yourself and share a number of ways to increase your music related revenue.

After we've talked about ways to make more money, we will cover how to properly manage your money to strategically position your business for growth. Lastly, I'll provide a straightforward explanation as to how to pay business taxes and which forms you need to complete to make sure you comply with the law. We'll conclude with the benefits of giving back and how giving can make a positive impact on your life.

So, let's get started with how to get paid from licensing your music.

Chapter 2: Get Paid Licensing Your Music

WHAT IS MUSIC LICENSING?

In my first book, *Start Your Music Business™*, I explained the different types of royalties that your music can earn. Well, it's not enough to simply understand the types of royalties available. You need to know how to formulate a *plan* to use that knowledge and convert it into music income. That is what music licensing is all about. Music licensing is the process of selling the rights to use your songs to other people and businesses as a means of making money.

Why Should You License Your Music?

Radio stations, television shows, restaurants, cruises, nightclubs, concerts, and other venues all want access to quality music. However, they typically are not in the business of writing and publishing songs. Instead, the songs that they use are usually songs that they have licensed, or paid a fee to the owners of the song, in exchange for the right to play the songs.

Licensing is a great way to put the songs that you have written, or purchased, to work for you. Instead of being a songwriter with a collection of great music that you have not done anything with, you can be a business owner that has a steady stream of income from royalties you earn from licensing your music. Another benefit to licensing your music is that the more successful you are, the more others will want to use your songs. This will also increase your music business income.

How to Build Your Own Music Catalog

The first thing you will need to do to get started with licensing your music is how to build your music catalog. A music catalog is a collection of songs that you own. Whenever you own music, you are legally entitled to the rights that come with ownership which include royalty income. Royalty income is the money that you earn from your songs every time someone uses the song with your permission. The process of allowing people to use your songs in exchange for a fee is called licensing. The more marketable the songs are that you own, the more you can potentially earn in royalty income.

Build Your Music Catalog by Writing Music

You can build your own music catalog by either (1) writing songs yourself or (2) purchasing the rights to songs from other songwriters. Writing your own music may be the least expensive way to build your catalog as it relates to money since the only real cost you will have is the expense associated with registering your ownership of the songs with the U.S. Copyright Office. This is very critical to protect your rights. I discuss the benefits of registering your music and the process to register your music in detail in my first book, *Start Your Music Business*™. Other than the cost related to registering your songs with the U.S. Copyright Office, you will be *investing* your time as a songwriter. You will need time to spend writing music and developing your skills as a songwriter. I refer to it as *investing* because there is still a cost associated with dedicating your time to something. For example, if you could normally earn $15/hour on your job, if it takes you 6 hours to write a song, you have invested $90 ($15 x 6 hours) worth of your earning potential to songwriting. This means that if it "costs" you $90 per song, but you could buy a better song from a more talented songwriter for $50, you may want to consider building your catalog by buying songs instead. Always track the amount of time you are spending as a songwriter by writing down how long you spent working on music so that you can know for sure if you are "breaking even" or losing money by writing songs yourself.

Build Your Music Catalog by Buying Music

Alternatively, you can choose to build your music catalog by buying music from other songwriters or producers. Finding music to buy is relatively simple. You can search via social media for music producers or songwriters and ask to hear samples of their work. You can also do online searches to find producers and songwriters with music for sale.

Here are a few things to consider before buying music:

1. **Ownership** – Make sure that the person you are buying music from actually owns the music. You should only buy songs that have been registered with the United States Copyright Office. I wrote about how to register a Copyright for your music in my first book, *Start Your Music Business*. You can check to see if the seller actually owns the music by searching for it on the United States Copyright Office website: www.copyright.gov

2. **Copyright** - Make sure you that you and the seller agree that the seller will assign (legally transfer) the copyright (ownership) of the music that you are buying to you. You will need to have a Copyright Assignment or Copyright Transfer Agreement drawn up. Our firm routinely prepares these for clients and you should be able to have one drafted very inexpensively.

3. **Record It** – You should file the Copyright Assignment or Transfer Agreement with the United States Copyright Office. Again, this is something a lawyer can assist you with in order to make sure that all of the rights have been properly assigned (given) to you and that the assignment complies with the law.

How to Collect Performance Royalties

Once you have built your catalog, by either writing music yourself or purchasing music, you will need to establish a system to license (legally give people permission to use your songs) and administer (manage and collect) the royalty payments generated by your collection. The first type of royalties we will discuss will be establishing a system to collect performance royalties. In the first book in the Music Law Series™ *Start Your Music Business*™, we discussed performance royalties so make sure you review the definition before we move forward.

What are Performing Rights Societies?

After you have built up a collection of songs in your music catalog, you may want to consider signing up for an account with a performing rights society. Performing rights societies are companies that license your music to other businesses and individuals that want to use your songs. There are two major companies that license music for songwriters and publishers: Broadcast Music, Inc. (BMI) and the American Society of Composers, Authors and Publishers (ASCAP).

How do Performing Rights Societies Collect and Pay Performance Royalties?

The first step to licensing music through a performing rights society is to register your catalog of songs with the performing rights societies. Businesses and individuals that want to license music pay performance royalties in exchange for the right to use your songs. The performing rights society then administers (collects) the payment and disburses (pays) it to the publisher and songwriter of the song.

Can you license music yourself if you are affiliated with BMI or ASCAP?

BMI and ASCAP do not have exclusive rights under their agreements. This means you can still license music yourself even if you are registered with them. You just need to let them know if you do so that they do not sue the venue thinking they are using your music for a public performance without paying you.

How to Register with a Performing Rights Society

Here is how you register:

Step One: Visit www.ascap.com or www.bmi.com (you can only register with one).

Step Two: Complete the application

Step Three: Pay the fee.

At the time of this printing, BMI charges $250 for publishers (LLC, corporation or partnership or $150 for individuals). ASCAP charges $25.

Step Four: Submit a publisher's clearance form. If your company is the only publisher, you should list that you will receive 100% of the publisher's share. If you have hired another publisher, you can divide the share based on the amount you agreed (e.g., 25% for the other publisher and 75% for you publisher).

For more information on the difference between publishers and writers, please reference the first book in the Music Law Series™ *Start Your Music Business*™.

If you would like to learn how to setup your own publishing company in order to receive 100% of your royalties, keep reading!

Step Five: Submit a writer's clearance form for each song. This form allows you to get paid. Make sure that all of the percentages add up to 100%. In you are in a band or a group, be sure to only include members of your group that co-wrote the song. If they are simply members of your group but did not participate in writing the song, you should not include them on the form. Instead, you can outline how they will be paid in a separate contract (e.g., a flat fee per performance, etc.).

For more information on how to divide income when multiple people participate in writing a song, please reference the first book in the Music Law Series™ *Start Your Music Business*™.

How to Setup Your Own Publishing Company

If you decide to be the songwriter and publisher (collect 100% of royalty income), then you will need to setup your own music publishing company.

Starting your own music publishing company generally consists of the following steps.

Step One: Search the available names on BMI or ASCAP. It is best to make sure that the name you want to use for your music publishing company is available before you go through the process of formally setting up a business with that name.

Step Two: Perform a Legal Name Search. After you have confirmed the name is available with BMI and ASCAP, I always recommend that you conduct a comprehensive legal name search to make sure that another company or individual does not own the rights to the name you would like to use for your publishing company. Again, this process is explained at length in book one of the Music Law Series™ *Start Your Music Business*™. However, it primarily means searching federal trademark registries, state trademark registries, company registries in all 50 states; common law claims, as well as web searches and domain name searches. My law firm routinely performs this service for clients and we recommend it as a way to make sure you do not get into legal trouble based on the name you are choosing to use for your business.

Step Three: Form a Company and apply for a Tax ID Number for the Business. (See my first book in the Music Law Series™ *Start Your Music Business*™ for benefits to setting up a company and steps for accomplishing this)

Step Four: Open an account with BMI or ASCAP. You can only register with one performing rights society so make sure you do your research before you make a decision. Check out the steps in this chapter for details on signing up.

Step Five: Open a business bank account in the name of your music publishing company that will be used to deposit your royalties.

Step Six: Copyright the songs with the U.S. Copyright Office. (See the first book in the Music Law Series™ *Start Your Music Business*™ for information regarding benefits as well as steps to take in order to register your music with the U.S. Copyright Office). If you have already previously registered the songs with the U.S. Copyright Office, make sure you have a lawyer prepare a Copyright Transfer or Copyright Assignment to legally transfer the ownership of your existing song to your newly formed music publishing company.

Step Seven: Register the songs that you own in your performing rights society account.

How to Setup Licensing Deals

Using a performing rights society to collect your performance royalties is a great way to make sure you are receiving income from licensing your music without the administrative tasks of having to manage it yourself. However, setting up an account to manage your royalties is just the first step. Once setup the account, you'll need to have a plan for actually getting buyers to license your music. You can accomplish this by (1) setting up licensing deals yourself or (2) hiring someone to shop your music around for you.

How to Contact Potential Buyers

Once you have your publishing company setup and your songs are properly registered under your publishing company, you can begin contacting potential buyers that may be interested in licensing your music directly. This will take effort, persistence and work on your part. However, it can be done if you are willing to have the discipline to form a *plan* and stick with it. Here are examples of plans you can execute to find people to license your music:

1. **Contact Local Artists** – You can research local artists that may want to use your songs. Pay attention to local artists that perform at restaurants, events at nightclubs featuring new talent, or even visit popular recording studios, music schools and universities. You can also discover local artists on social media sites.

2. **Contact Companies**- You can research companies that may take an interest in music you have written or own. Most hotels and restaurants license music to play in their elevators and lobby areas. Other businesses license music for commercials and promotional purposes.

3. **Contact Record Labels** – You can research independent record labels that may have artists that would be interested in the music you have available in your catalog. Research artists that may be interested in the kind of music you own and look up the record label that is listed on their album. You can then contact their agent or manager as a means of pitching your music to them.

4. **Contact Television Shows** - In addition, you can research and contact executive producers of television shows or music supervisors that select music for movies and pitch your music to them for licensing. Many of these companies are interested in new and undiscovered independent talent as the licensing fees are less expensive than established marquee artists. You can find their contact information by visiting company websites, social media pages, internet searches, attending industry conferences and workshops, researching film and movie credits, etc.

Negotiating Licensing Deals Yourself

The third and final step to setting up your own licensing deals is negotiating the terms. Once you have contacted the buyer and they are interested in licensing some of your music, you need a signed agreement outlining the terms. Here are three (3) common ways you can structure your licensing deals:

1. **Flat Fee:** You can set a price per number of units manufactured. For example, charge $100/song per 1,000 units manufactured. This means that for $100, the purchaser can reproduce 1,000 copies of the song. After that number is reached, they would have to contact you to pay again or negotiate new terms for more units. Alternatively, if you are selling songs to larger companies (e.g., a video game company) they typically pay between $2,000-5,000 per song.

2. **Flat Fee + Incentives.** You can structure the deal so that you receive an up-front flat fee of $3,000 to license the song plus an additional $2,000 based on the purchaser reaching certain sales benchmarks. Again, be sure to have this in writing.

3. **Work for hire.** You give up all rights to your ownership in the song forever. Many television studios want to exclusively make changes without having to consult you. If you choose this option, make sure the payment is worth the income you plan to receive for the lifetime of the song if you chose to license it rather than sell it outright.

Again, it is worth it to have a custom agreement drafted by your own attorney that you can use for your music business. Otherwise, the person that drafted the contract, (typically the other person's lawyer), will have likely drafted it with terms that will help the buyer – not you.

If the buyer does give you their licensing contract to sign, at least hire your own attorney to review the contract before you sign it to make sure it says what you think it does.

Hire Professionals to "Shop" Your Music.

You do not have to do everything alone. Another way to set up your own licensing deals is to hire someone that will focus on introducing your music, or shopping your music around to people within the music industry that may be interested in licensing your songs. This person is typically called an Administrator. An administrator will allow you to keep 100% ownership of your copyrights while shopping your song catalog around for a limited period of time to people that may be interested in licensing your music. In exchange for their services, you typically pay them a percentage of your royalty income plus a percentage of the up-front flat fee you receive for each placement. Administrators usually charge 10%-15% for their services. They meet with producers in studios, have lunch with A&R agents from record labels, contact record companies, and use their music industry contacts to promote your music.

Some administrators will also work with you under a Co-publishing arrangement. Instead of paying them a fee, you agree to transfer 50% of your copyright for the life of the copyright to them in exchange for their services. I highly recommend speaking with a lawyer and having an attorney draft a proper contract that will make sure that the person you hire does the work and you are not just giving away your copyright for free without the administrator ever securing any placements or licensing deals for you.

When considering hiring someone to shop your music around, you want to ask for references. Ask them how many placements they were successfully able to secure for their past clients and ask them how much those deals were worth. Then ask them for references (names and numbers of people they have worked with in the past) and contact those people. Ask their past clients if they were happy with the administrator's work and if they would hire them again. Most importantly, make sure that they actually have music industry contacts. Ask them to tell you specifically who they would contact and what they would expect to accomplish in the first 30 days of working with you. Lastly, make sure they respond to you. If they have trouble getting back to you before they have your money, you may not hear from them once they have it.

Here are a few companies you can contact about licensing your music for you:

Ocelot Music   http://www.ocelotmusic.com/

Rumblefish   www.Rumblefish.com

Remember, these are just suggestions to get you started. Make sure you interview companies yourself before you decide to do business with them. I'm not personally involved with these companies so be sure to do your own homework.

How to find people to help you.

If you decide that you prefer to hire someone that can help you get licensing deals for your songs, paying a percentage of your income in exchange for earning more money than you could make by your own efforts makes sense. Meaning, if you are a talented songwriter, hiring someone that already has contacts within the music industry to (1) shop your music to have your songs placed on albums released by major artists so that you can receive more royalty payments or (2) shop your music so that a major record label will sign you may be a great strategic move for your music business.

The best way to find these types of qualified individuals is to go places where they would be and ask people if they know of anyone that offers these services. Here are a few examples of places that you can go in order to ask for a qualified referral:

1. Music Stores

2. Studio sessions

3. Music Schools & Universities

4. Music Conferences

5. Join organizations and meet speakers:

6. ASCAP and BMI events

7. Music Association events

8. Music Publisher events

Once you find a potential administrator, make sure you follow the earlier tips in this chapter by negotiating how much you will have to pay them, asking for references, contacting those references, asking for their plan of action once you hire them, and making sure they have enough time to devote to your music and will respond to you when you reach out to them.

How to Earn Royalties from Compulsory Licenses

In addition to performance royalties, you can earn mechanical royalties from licensing your music. My first book in the Music Law™ series, *Start Your Music Business*™, goes into detail regarding the difference between performance royalties and mechanical royalties and ways to license your music in order to earn mechanical royalties.

To summarize it, the Copyright Act states that if a copyright owner distributes their musical recording to the public (other than a theatrical production) anyone else can distribute the recording after they give notice and pay the statutory rate (currently 9.10 cents per minute).

The rules are very specific and detailed. However, if an individual follows them, and makes the required royalty payments to the owner, they can obtain a compulsory license to use a song.

How to Collect Mechanical Royalties from Your Music

You can register with a company such as the Harry Fox Agency (www.HarryFox.com) to issue and manage any mechanical licensing requests you receive. The Harry Fox Agency typically charges 6.75% of income received plus an annual fee that ranges from $200-$800/year for this service.

Now that we have discussed how to make money from licensing deals, let's discuss some of the common types of contracts you will encounter in the music business and how to negotiate the best terms.

Chapter 3: Producer Agreements

You're more than a songwriter, producer, artist, or musician. You are a business owner and the success of your music business will largely be determined by the types of deals that you negotiate for your services. In the next few chapters, I'm going to discuss a few of the most common contracts you will encounter while building your music business and share with you key terms that you want to negotiate in order to win.

What are Producer Agreements?

Producer agreements are contracts that music producers sign with record labels or independent artists in which the music producer agrees to produce music for the record label or independent artist in exchange for payment and/or royalties.

Why You Need One?

Even if you're just making music out of your bedroom for your friends, you owe it to yourself to have a producer agreement in writing that you use with anyone that buys your beats or music. Producer agreements allow you to spell out the rights that you deserve to make sure you are not taken advantage of later.

Even if you are not a producer, if you have started your own record label or you are an independent artist, you still want to make sure you always have a written producer agreement any time you buy music or tracks from a producer for the same reasons. Without a contract that shows that you both agreed to certain terms, each person can claim something different. This could easily end with you losing royalties, rights, credit or even money. However, the good news is, once you have a good producer agreement, you can likely use the same agreement for almost all of your deals by simply revising or updating the contract information.

When should you mention the Producer Agreement?

Like most contracts, the best time to bring up your agreement is before you ever start doing work. You should have your producer agreement with you at your first meeting with a prospective buyer so that they can have an opportunity to review it and sign it before you start working on their music.

Having a professional producer agreement will show your clients that you are serious about your music business and the work that you do as a producer. It will also let you know which clients are serious about themselves and their music business.

Having a producer agreement also makes sure that your buyer understands how much money they're promising to pay you as well as who owns the rights to the songs before the record is made. It is common for people to develop amnesia and forget the amounts that they promised to pay you as well as the rights that you are entitled to receive once the project is completed and the song files have been transferred. If you make it a habit to have a signed agreement on file up front, it can save you from legal fees later on.

Standard Terms of Producer Agreements

Most producer agreements include several terms (conditions) and clauses that have legal significance. Depending on your situation, you can often negotiate other terms that are in your best interest. Some examples of a few of the terms that you may see in a producer agreement include:

1. **The parties.** This clause (paragraph) lets you know who the key players are in the contract. For example, most producer agreements are between the producer and the record label that is hiring them to produce a track or entire record. However, the contract may also be between the producer and an independent artist that hired them directly.

2. **Services.** This clause will let you know what the record label or independent artist is paying you to do. For example, it may say that you are responsible for producing one master recording or an entire

album. It may even spell out specific tasks such as: *supervising rehearsals, booth and studio work at recording sessions, mastering, dubbing, editing, mixing, and re-editing for single record versions.* I recommend that you make sure that the services listed are the actual services that you are willing to perform for the price agreed. You don't want the artist or label to later argue that you are supposed to do more for the money they paid you because you left this section blank or did not include everything.

3. **Producer royalty**. This clause will tell you the exact amount that you will receive per song or per record sold. It is usually written as a percentage (e.g., 3%).

4. **Producer Advance**. Typically, the record label will give the producer a cash advance based on the label's budget for the album. The producer then records the album and agrees to assign (give) ownership of the final product, the master sound recording (actual recording) to the record label. The record label then distributes the album for sale. The initial royalties that belong to the artist from the album sales will be used to recoup (repay) the money the label "loaned" the artist for recording costs. This "loan" is typically called an advance. After the recording costs are recouped by the label, the label will then use the producer royalties to recoup (repay) the producer advance. THEN, once the producer advance has been

recouped (repaid), the producer will begin to earn royalties on each record sold.

5. **Ownership.** Most producer agreements will say that the record label will keep the entire ownership of the sound recording when your sessions are completed. Many labels will also request ownership of all work associated with each recording session.

6. **Samples.** The agreement may include a policy against using samples in the music without the record label giving their permission. If you are a producer that has used samples, make sure the contract spells out who is responsible for clearing the samples and the associated expense. In my first book in the Music Law Series™, *Start Your Music Business*™, I have an entire chapter dedicated to clearing samples legally. Make sure you check it out if you are planning to use samples in the music you produce.

7. **Publishing / Split Sheet.** This sheet will outline the percentage of ownership that you will have in the song as a producer based on your contributions. It will also list other co-producers that are entitled to royalties as well as the artist and their management. I also explain split sheets in *Start Your Music Business*™ and other tips for making sure that you are paid what you deserve when you make music or collaborate with other people.

8. **Letter of Direction.** This letter may be attached to the agreement and usually gives rights or authority to another party. For example, a record label may include a Letter of Direction giving Sound Exchange permission to collect and provide digital royalties directly to you.

What are Key Terms you Should Negotiate?

With every contract, there are terms or promises the parties have agreed to that are included. If you want to grow your music business, you must be willing to negotiate or ask for terms other than the ones that are included in the contract you receive. Negotiation is a skill because if it is not done correctly, you may lose the opportunity altogether. It may be best to leave the negotiations to a professional such as your manager, agent or attorney if you do not feel comfortable asking for things from other people. However, here are some general terms that you may want to negotiate within your producer agreement:

1. **Negotiate the Royalty.** If you are the producer, ask for a higher royalty percentage. Higher royalties are usually paid to producers with resumes of impressive placements and talent.

If you are the record label or artist, you probably want to negotiate to pay the producer the least amount possible. Industry standard typically starts at 3% so it would be in your best interest to only pay the producer that amount or no royalty at all and just give them a one-time flat fee.

2. **Negotiate Credit.** Make sure that you receive producer credit (your name listed as the producer on the record and all other marketing material). This will help establish your reputation in the industry and attract more clients that will want to hire you.

3. **Negotiate Royalty Terms.** If you are a producer, you will want to make sure you receive royalties from other exploitation (uses of the record) including music videos, film, sync agreements, television and advertising.

If you are the artist or record label, you may want to limit the amount that the producer can participate in royalties from your other sources of revenue.

4. **Negotiate your advance.** If you are a producer, you may want to ask for a larger producer advance if you feel that the song is in high demand or that the record label or artist can afford more. Also, make sure the advance is non-returnable (that you will not have to pay it back if the album does not sell).

As a record label or artist, you likely want to negotiate that you do not have to pay an advance altogether or that the advance is as reasonable or low as possible to stay within your album budget.

5. **Negotiate Publishing.** As a producer, it is in your best interest to receive the largest share of publishing ownership that you can

based on your actual contributions (e.g., 50%, 25%, etc.). Record labels and artists will often try and lower your share without having legitimately contributed to the production of the music. Make sure the publishing splits reflected in the Producer Agreement match the splits that all of the contributing parties signed and agreed to on the actual Split Sheets. If you are not familiar with Split Sheets or how to create one, please reference my book *Start Your Music Business*™.

6. **Audit Rights.** Producers, make sure you have the right to audit (examine) the financial records of the record label or artist that hired you to make sure you are receiving the royalties you are entitled to receive. Unfortunately, some people will be unfair and simply not report all of the sales. You can have it written into your contracts that they are legally obligated to give you opportunities to take a look at the financials (or have your accountant or attorney look at them for you) in order to make sure that you are being paid what you deserve.

If you are the record label or independent artist, you will want to limit this right by making sure they have to travel to your office or place of business to look at the records, that they are required to give you advance notice (7 business days) before asking to see the records, and that if they do not dispute or raise an issue with the royalty statements after one year, they lose their right to do it in the future. These clauses will help you avoid having a producer from several years back coming after you in court for a mistake that was made and not brought to your attention in a timely fashion.

7. **Samples.** As a producer, make sure you understand the record label or independent artist's position on samples *before* you use them in your music. You may want to negotiate terms that require the record label to be financially responsible for clearing any samples.

If you are the artist or record label hiring the producer, you will want the producer to be fully responsible for clearing (paying to get legal permission to use) samples. Make sure you have your attorney draft specific language that makes the producer liable (legally and financially responsible) for any lawsuits that arise as a result of them not clearing the samples properly.

8. **Control Your Image.** As a producer, you may want to limit the record label's use of your likeness (image) to activities relating to selling the album. You may not want to give away the right to use your name, photos and biography forever – as it may limit your control over your brand. Instead, you can negotiate that they can use your likeness for a limited period of time (5 or 10 years) in association with promoting the album. However, after that timeframe, they will need to ask your permission.

Unfortunately, I know too many small companies that associated with an artist or producer before they became famous and still use that person's image to promote their business years later – even though that person is no longer affiliated with them.

If you are the record label or independent artist that hired the producer, you will want to negotiate that you get the right to use their likeness and image for as long as possible. They could become the next big producer and your association with them could help your industry reputation.

9. **Miscellaneous** – There will undoubtedly be a number of other terms and clauses within the agreement that we have not covered. In my years of practice, I have encountered some producer agreements that "snuck in" completely one-sided clauses in order to cheat the producer or the record label (depending on whose attorney prepared the contract). I always recommend that you have an experienced attorney review your agreement line by line to make sure that it says exactly what you and the other person have agreed that it should say.

Chapter 4: Songwriter Agreements

Now that we understand the basics of producer agreements, let's discuss songwriter agreements. A songwriter agreement is used when someone wants to buy a song or multiple songs from a person that writes songs. In exchange for giving up all or some of the ownership of the songs, the writer is paid a flat fee or a percentage of the income earned from the sale of the songs (sometimes both).

Types of Songwriter Agreements

There are several different types of songwriter agreements. Here are some of the most common types of agreements you may encounter in the music industry:

1. **Exclusive Agreement.** The songwriter agrees to assign or give the rights to all of the songs that they write within a period of time to the purchaser. In exchange, the purchaser agrees to pay the songwriter some of the income earned from the song. Songwriters

can also negotiate that the buyer pays them an advance (amount up front before any songs are even sold).

2. **Individual Song Agreement.** This contract allows the songwriter to sell the rights to one song to a purchaser in exchange for a share of the income from the song. The songwriter can also accept a flat fee in exchange for the rights to the song or a combination of both.

3. **Co-Publishing Agreement** – The songwriter agrees to share the ownership of the song, share the publisher's share of the song income, and completely keep the writer's share of the song income. This is a great way to give your publisher an incentive to find a good placement for your song on someone's album, without having to give up all of your rights to your song.

4. **Administration Agreement** – As a songwriter, you can also sign with a publishing company that has existing relationships within the music industry. The publishing company will agree to exploit, or "shop around" your music by introducing it to various artists, producers, and record labels in hopes of getting you a placement on an album. In exchange for their services, the publisher would be entitled to a percentage of income earned from the song. This can be a great way to get your music in the hands of the right people without having to sacrifice your ownership in your music.

Songwriters want placements, or to have their song purchased by popular artists and placed as a song on albums. This is how songwriters make money. Even if you are talented, you simply may not have the industry contacts you need to reach the types of artists that you want to hear your music. Therefore, having a publisher with industry connections may be the best thing.

What are Key Terms in Songwriter Agreements?

Songwriter agreements have a number of terms that you should be aware of before signing on the dotted line. Again, I certainly cannot cover them all. However, here are some examples of just a few of the terms you may see:

1. **The parties.** Same as above.

2. **Services.** This clause will tell you how many songs you are committed to providing for the price you are being paid. Make sure you review this carefully and have everything that you are committing to do included in writing so that the buyer cannot argue later that you told them you would do something else.

3. **Term.** This clause lets you know how long you are agreeing to provide services for the buyer. You may be required to write songs for a specific period of time (e.g., one year) or the contract may be to purchase only one song.

4. **Ownership.** Most songwriter agreements will say that the songwriter will assign (give) the entire copyright (ownership) of the song to the purchaser. This clause may also say that all of the songs you have written previously will belong to the buyer.

I have seen this language in industry contracts many times. The songwriter thought they were selling one song when really they were agreeing to legally give the buyer all of the songs they had ever written! This is why I always encourage songwriters to have a lawyer review your contracts before you sign them. Saving a few hundred dollars by not hiring me would have cost my client the value of his entire song catalog since he had read the contract himself and did not even know this clause was in it!

5. **Exclusive.** This clause will tell you who you can write songs for. The contract may say that you can only write songs for the buyer during the term (for example, you only write songs for this particular record label for the entire year).

The contract may also say that only the buyer can use the song and you cannot sell it to anyone else. In both of these scenarios, this would mean that the contract is an "exclusive agreement".

A "non-exclusive agreement" gives you the flexibility to write songs for other people during the term (time period) of the contract or license the same song to other people in addition to the buyer.

6. **Royalty Income.** This clause will tell you how much you as the songwriter will earn from royalty income. For example, the contract may state that you will receive 50% of royalty income (mechanical, synchronization, print income).

7. **Assignment of Copyright.** The contract will also usually include a form for you to sign to assign (transfer) the ownership of the copyright to the purchaser.

8. **Right of First Refusal.** If your copyrights expire by law, the purchaser may include language that gives them the "right of first refusal" or option to get ownership of your copyrights before anyone else.

9. **Miscellaneous** – There will undoubtedly be a number of other terms and clauses within the agreement. Again, make sure you have your agreement reviewed by your own lawyer to legally interpret the other terms and conditions to make sure that the agreement says exactly what you believe it should say.

What are Key Terms you Should Negotiate?

Every deal is different and there are a number of ways to negotiate a Songwriter Agreement depending on the terms and the bargaining position of the parties. However, here are just a few examples of things you can negotiate:

1. **Copyrights.** If you are the songwriter, try to keep ownership of the song and just license (give them permission) to use the song for a period of time. This will allow you to keep the song in your catalog and perhaps find future ways to license and make money from it.

    If you are buying the song, you will want to negotiate that you own 100% of it for the price you are paying – or as much of it as the songwriter will agree.

2. **Past Work.** If you are the songwriter, you may want to negotiate to keep the rights to previous songs you have written. Out of desperation, some songwriters will sign over their entire catalog since their old material did not make many sales. They oftentimes overlook the fact that the new exposure they will receive from licensing their new music will likely cause sales for their older music to increase as they gain name recognition. For example, have you ever learned about a new artist and then went back and bought all of their older music? Therefore, it may be in your best interest to keep the rights to the songs you have written in the past.

    If you are the buyer, I still don't recommend that you sneak this clause in. Instead, if you want to own a songwriter's entire catalog, make them a fair offer for it and make sure they know up front that this is in the contract. It's the right thing to do. Your reputation in the music industry is important and being the type of person that cheats people may keep good songwriters from wanting to do business with you in the future.

3. **Credit.** Songwriters, you may want to negotiate a clause that requires the purchaser to include you as the writer of the song in any promotions. Even if you have sold your ownership, this additional marketing will help build your brand in the music industry and may lead to more business.

4. **Advance.** Songwriters, you may want to negotiate a clause that requires the purchaser to give you an advance (or negotiate a larger advance). You will also want to make sure that you do not have to pay it back if the song does not sell.

   If you are buying the song, you will want to keep your expenses as low as possible which means not paying the songwriter an advance or paying them the lowest advance possible.

5. **Publishing.** Songwriters, you may want to negotiate to receive the largest share of publishing ownership possible based on your actual contributions (e.g., 50%, 25%, etc.) For example, if you wrote the entire song, don't allow the buyer to convince you to only accept a 50% share of ownership when you should receive 100%.

   Some buyers choose to try and negotiate to receive a percentage of publishing from the songwriter although they did not contribute to writing the song. I'm personally not in favor of this and feel that buyers can fairly make their money by exploiting (marketing) the song while still allowing the songwriter to keep their rightful share of royalty income in the song they have written. However, if you are the buyer and have contributed to writing the song, by all means negotiate to get your percentage of the writer's share.

6. **Audits.** Songwriters, you may want to make sure that you negotiate a clause that gives you the right to audit the financial records of the buyer to make sure you are receiving the royalties you are entitled to receive. In business, you do not want to just rely on people's "word." Instead, have your rights spelled out in writing so that you can legally enforce and receive what you are entitled to if they decide not to abide by the contract in the future.

7. **Moral Rights.** Songwriters, ask for moral rights. Moral rights means that the purchaser has to get your permission before they change or alter the song. This can help protect your reputation as a songwriter and will make sure the final version of the song is still something that you are proud to be affiliated with.

If you are the buyer, you may not want to give away moral rights because you will likely want the ability to change the song without having to constantly get permission from the songwriter.

8. **Right of Reversion.** Songwriters, you may want to consider including a right of reversion clause that states that if the buyer does not use the song within a specific time-frame, you get to reclaim the ownership rights. Make sure this language is properly drafted to comply with your state's laws.

    If you're buying the song, you absolutely would want to negotiate to leave this clause out of your agreement as not having it in the contract would give you the option to sell the song to someone else if you were not able to use it instead of having to give it back to the songwriter.

9. **Income.** Songwriters, if you decide not to negotiate any of the above key terms, make sure that you ask to increase the flat fee and ask for more royalties in exchange for the rights that you are losing.

10. **Non-Exclusive.** Songwriters, you should usually negotiate to keep the option to license the song to other people as well. This is not always an option so if the buyer is asking to be the only one able to use the song (exclusive agreement) or is asking you to only write songs for them, then be sure to negotiate and increase the price.

    Buyers will usually want to negotiate the rights to the song are exclusive so that the artists on your record label are the only individuals able to use the song and you do not have to worry about hearing it on someone else's album or website.

11. **Other Clauses.** Depending on the other clauses included within the agreement, make sure you understand their legal significance and negotiate them in order to enter the best deal possible.

Now that we understand the basics of songwriter agreements, let's discuss recording artist agreements.

Chapter 5: Recording Artist Agreements

The last type of agreement we will discuss is called a recording artist agreement. Many artists want to be signed as an artist under a major record label. This means that the artist has signed a specially drafted contract called a recording artist agreement provided by the record label which gives the label certain rights to the artist's music and gives the artist certain benefits due to their affiliation with the label. Let's explore this important agreement in more detail.

Why do Artists Sign with Record Labels?

Artists often think that signing with a record label means they will have a team of people that schedule their tours, book their promotional events, market their albums on television, the internet and in stores, and handle the entire business end of their career. They envision having access to the best producers and musicians while they simply focus on making quality music and collecting their royalty checks.

In some instances, this may be the case. However, in order for a recording artist agreement to be beneficial for an independent artist, (1) the label needs to be able to add value to the artist's music career; and (2) the terms of the recording artist agreement need to match the promises that the label made to the artist . Let's explore these two points in detail.

How Record Labels Add Value to Artists

There are many different record labels and they vary in both size and resources. In order for an independent artist to know if signing with a particular record label is in their best interests, they need to know the benefits or "value" the label can add to their current music business.

With the internet, there are many resources that artists are able to take advantage of themselves without the help of a major label. It's important that the label offers benefits in one of these key areas above and beyond what you can reasonably do for yourself as an artist in order to make it worth the rights (potential revenue) that you will give up by signing. Here are a few ways that a label may be able to add value to an independent artist:

1. **Distribution.** This means the label may be able to get your music sold in physical stores and/or online stores. You will want to look into this by looking at other artists on the label to see where their music is being sold. If their music is only available on iTunes® and you already know how to get your music on iTunes®, then it may

not be beneficial for you to give up a portion of your music related revenue to the label for something you can already do for yourself.

On the contrary, if all of their artists are being sold in major stores as well as overseas and you do not currently have the means to accomplish this, then signing with this particular label may be worth considering.

2. **Access to Talent.** The label may be able to give you access to high-profile and talented individuals to assist with your albums. Their roster of talent may include other famous artists that may be willing to be featured on your album, popular producers, musicians, vocalists, graphic designers, videographers, photographers, makeup artists, image consultants, etc.,

Again, you will need to confirm that the label really has these connections. One way to accomplish this is by taking a look at the credits on previous albums that artists on the label have released. If they feature renown individuals, then perhaps the label will have the connections to get similar people involved with your project.

3. **Financial support (loans).** Most labels are run like businesses and don't do anything for free. The clothes, travel, cars, etc. that newly signed artists buy are likely paid with advances (loans) from the label that must be repaid (recouped) from future music revenue.

For example, the label may provide you with financial support (loans) to cover standard album costs. Typical costs that the label may cover may include:

- Production (recording costs including producer's advance(s))
- Artwork costs
- Studio rentals
- Engineering, mixing (and remixing), editing, and mastering
- Instrument rental
- Transportation, hotel accommodations, wardrobe stipends, meals, etc.

However, these loans generally must be repaid and the label must be reimbursed for their costs before you begin to make money from your music.

4. **Booking.** The label may provide you with booking support by handling booking requests and booking shows and tours.

   Again, you will need to pay careful attention to which costs the label is covering, how much of the money you make will go to the label, and which costs must be repaid. You will also want to see if the label is simply providing booking support (processing requests, scheduling your travel, etc.) versus actually marketing to promoters to book shows and tours for you.

5. **Exposure.** The label may provide you with increased exposure and marketing (e.g., interviews in magazines, blogs, television shows, radio airplay, etc.)

   However, you will want to be sure that the label has real connections with radio stations and has had airplay for its artists in the past. Otherwise, they may be hoping to simply get a cut of your existing sales without increasing your fanbase through exposure.

How to Know if Your Label Can Deliver

As I shared earlier, a label needs to be able to add value to your music career as an artist in order for it to be worth it for you to give up a share of your music related income. I've listed a few of the main ways that a label could add value to your music career as an artist. However, how do you know if a label really can deliver on those promises? Meaning, most labels will tell you they can get your music on the radio and that they have top producers that will work with you. They may also promise that your schedule will be full of shows and tours that they will arrange. But how do you know for sure if they really can perform or if those are just promises to get you to sign on the dotted line? Here are a few suggestions to help you research the label in order to know if the offer is worth signing:

1. **Interview Artists.** The first thing you will want to do is talk to the other artists on the label. Ask your contact at the label if they can

give you contact information to some of the other artists. If they are unwilling to do this, they may have something to hide. Here are the questions you want to ask the other artists:

- How many units did their last EP or album sell?

- How many shows did they do in the last year?

- How many tours did they go on?

- Did the label book those opportunities for them or did they get them from their existing fanbase?

- Are they able to support themselves full-time with the income they're making from their music or do they have to work outside jobs?

- How much did they make last year? (It's worth asking. They may not be comfortable answering but it's worth a try. You can also try to get them to give you a range (between $45-$50,000)

- What was the last royalty check they received from the label? How much was it?

- How long did it take the label to release their album?

- Did they feel the label provided sufficient marketing for their project? (interviews, etc.)

- Do they feel the label has helped their music get airplay and/or exposure?

- Would they sign if they had a chance to do it all over again?

Keep in mind that some artists on the label may not be honest. They may feel that they signed a bad deal and may want everyone else to make the same mistake. Or, they may simply be covering for the label. This is why you will want to interview as many of the artists as possible on the label. Once you have interviewed them, confirm the information they give. Most artists' websites list their upcoming and past shows. This is just one way to see how much work they are getting. You can also compare this information to the facts you learn from researching the label to make sure it all adds up.

2. **Interview Management.** Next, you'll want to talk to as many individuals in management as possible. You can ask them questions like:

    1. *What are the goals of the label for the next 5 years?* You want to hear them outline a defined plan for growing their

fanbase and getting more media exposure which will result in you earning more music income if you sign with them.

2. *What specific steps will the label take to market your future albums?* You want to hear them speak of specific contacts that they have used in the past that will get you interviews, radio airplay, promotional events, and exposure.

3. *How much can you expect to make each year from your music?* You want to know that after they deduct their percentages that you will be making more from your music with the label than you did before you signed.

4. *How much did the other artists on their label earn from royalties last year?*

5. *How much did the other artists on their label earn from album sales last year?*

6. *How many shows and tours did the label book for the other artists on their label last year?* Again, you want to make sure that they will be providing a benefit to you which means giving you more shows than what you are currently booking on your own.

7. *How will royalty splits work? What percentage of your music income will the label be keeping for themselves?*

8. *How much will you earn from merchandise, shows and tours?* You want to make sure that you get to keep as much of this revenue as possible. Preferably 100% since the label often tries to keep as much of your album sales as possible.

3. **General Research.** You also want to confirm the information the artists and management shared with you by fact-checking. This means that if they said that they performed a show at a large venue, you contact the venue to confirm it occurred and perhaps find out how many people attended. You can look at their website and albums to confirm features and producers that have worked on the project. Also visit local stores to see if their albums are on the shelves or if you hear their songs on relevant radio stations. The goal is to make sure that they are a legitimate company with the industry contacts and resources to actually help your music career instead of simply taking a percentage of the existing income that you are making. Record labels are a business and it is important that you as an artist protect your legal interests in the process.

What are the Disadvantages of Signing with a Label?

Now that we understand the value that a record label can potentially add to your music career and ways to confirm if they can actually deliver on those promises, we need to discuss what you may have to give up. Meaning, if you have concluded that the label can enhance your existing music business by exposing you to more fans and helping you make more revenue through shows, tours and merchandise, you will need to see if those benefits outweigh the costs of signing with them.

1. **Loss of Song Ownership.** You may lose ownership of all of the songs you have written in the past as well as songs you write while under contract with the label. As an artist, it is in your best interests to negotiate that you get to keep all of your rights to your songs.

    This may not be realistic depending on how successful the label is and the level of exposure they can offer you. The more successful the label and its current roster of artists are, the more difficult it may be for you to keep the rights to your music. However, a skilled attorney should be able to assist with this. As a worst case scenario, you should try to negotiate that you only have to give up ownership of new material that you write while under contract with the label – not your previous works.

2. **Loss of album sale income.** When you're independent, if you sell an album for $10, you get to keep the entire $10 minus sales tax and any other taxes. Once you sign with a record label, they will try their best to keep the majority of the $10. Here's how they do it.

Most recording artist agreements will allow the label to recoup any funds they advanced to you for recording costs. This means whenever someone buys your album, they label will continue keeping the entire $10 from album sales (minus their distribution costs, etc.) until the $20,000+ they may have spent on production costs, marketing, etc. for your album is repaid. Instead, you'll likely earn less than $.10 per album as a royalty unless you negotiate more.

> I often let my clients know that as an independent artist, they can sell 4,000 units (albums) at $10 each and make $40,000 for the year. Or, as a signed artist, they would need to sell *400,000* albums if they earned $.10 per album to make $40,000 in one year. Again, terms vary but most recording artist agreements are structured to allow the record label to keep the majority of the revenue made from album sales.

How Do Signed Artists Make Money?

Your income as a signed recording artist will typically be limited to shows, touring, and merchandise until you are popular enough to demand better terms. Sadly, this may not be enough income to support you full-time. That is why it is important to research the record label before you sign with them to make sure they have the industry connections to grow your fanbase so that you can book enough shows and tours to make a living.

Otherwise, if you sign with a small label or one that is large but is not committed to giving you support, you may find yourself still doing the same amount of work booking your own shows while having lost your album sale income.

How Can Artists Protect Themselves

As I shared at the beginning of this chapter, independent artists can protect themselves by researching to make sure (1) the label is able to add value to the artist's music career; and (2) the terms of the recording artist agreement match the promises that the label made to the artist. Let's explore the last point about the contract itself.

Regardless of what the label representatives tell you, you need to be certain that you understand the document you are signing and that the legal information within that contract matches the promises the label made to you. It is easy for label representatives to verbally sell you on the promise of album sales, national tours, merchandise revenue, fame and fortune.

However, if those "promises" are not spelled out in the agreement you sign, you typically cannot enforce them because most contracts include clauses that keep you from bringing in outside terms that are not included in the final document. There are certain legal exceptions to this of course but they can be costly and difficult to prove.

How do Major Recording Artists End up Broke?

Historically, many famous artists have been taken advantage of by record labels simply because they did not truly understand the recording artist agreement they signed. Perhaps they were told one thing, but the contract required them to give up more rights than they bargained for. This dramatically reduced the earnings they were entitled to from their album sales. This is why you sometimes hear of major artists that have sold thousands if not millions of albums, but have to file for bankruptcy.

Therefore, it is important that you as an artist make sure you *completely* understand every term in the contract before you sign it. Let's discuss some of the most common terms within the recording artist agreement:

Key Terms in Recording Artist Agreements

1. **Commitment.** Most recording artist agreements begin by telling you what you are required to do under the contract which is called your "commitment". For example, the label may ask you to record two full-length albums for three years or provide 10 masters per year. It may also give deadlines for submitting the albums (e.g., first album due within 8 months of signing the contract).

The label may even require that you make a Greatest Hits album with your music. You will need to make sure you understand exactly what will be required for you to fulfill your commitment to the label under the contract. Anytime you consider recording something, you will want to make sure that it counts toward your commitment (for example, most Greatest Hits albums typically do not count toward the commitment unless you negotiate otherwise).

2. **Your Music.** The recording artist agreement may say that you cannot use music you have already recorded to fulfill your commitment (recording obligations) to the label. This means you will need to record new music to fulfill your agreement with the label unless you negotiate otherwise.

3. **Label Approval.** Most recording artist agreements will say that recordings must be to the label's satisfaction. This means you will have to keep recording the album until it is to their satisfaction in order for it to count toward fulfilling your recording commitment.

4. **Delivery.** There may also be a requirement that you give everything to the label after recording (Masters, tracks, sessions, vocals, etc.) and they will of course keep the rights. This means you may want to limit the music you record during your studio

sessions to work specifically geared toward your commitment to the label or they may end up owning the recordings.

5. **Use of Songs.** When your recording artist agreement with the label ends, the contract may limit you from recording any songs you recorded while under contract with them for a period of time (typically 5 years) after you give the Master recording to them.

6. **Samples.** The recording artist agreement may say that the label must approve any samples that you use if you want the song to count toward fulfilling your commitment. You may have to pay for getting proper clearances for samples you use in your music yourself. Make sure you read this section carefully. For a complete discussion on how to clear samples, feel free to reference my first book *Start Your Music Business*™.

7. **Term.** The recording artist agreement will say how long you are agreeing to work for the label.

8. **Renewals.** The recording artist agreement may say that it will automatically renew. This means the label can extend your contract without your permission.

9. **Exclusive.** Recording artist agreements often say that you cannot work for any other label or take on other music commitments without the label's permission. Again, this is why it is important

to make sure the label will have the resources to provide you with enough music related income to make up for the fact that you may be restricted from taking advantage of other opportunities in the music business while you are with the label.

10. **Ownership of Works.** Recording artist agreements often say that the label will own the rights to songs you wrote both while you are under contract as well as songs you wrote before the contract. The label will typically state that they own all masters and the right to duplicate your songs forever as well as will own the sound recording rights and will be the sole owner of all worldwide rights in and to each audiovisual record.

11. **Moral Rights.** The recording artist agreement may also say that you waive any moral rights. This means that the label will be able to change or alter your songs and performances without your permission.

12. **Lawsuit.** Recording artist agreements will typically say that if you end up suing the label in court, you do not have the right to sue to end the contract. Instead you can sue to get the royalties you are owed but you would still have to fulfill your recording commitment to the label.

For example, if the label breaks the agreement in some way, instead of you being able to sue to get out of the contract, you would still have to finish out the contract and the label would instead have to pay back the money they owed you. But, they would still get to keep you under contract.

13. **Royalties.** The recording artist agreements may say that the royalties you will earn will vary from 5-10% of the actual wholesale price minus discounts, taxes or gross revenue received minus all costs. Record labels will often state that they will only have to pay you 75% of the minimum statutory royalty rate for songs you write. Again, make sure you have your own attorney explain the meaning of these sections in the agreement since they are different in each contract.

14. **Promotional Performances.** They may also include a clause stating that they do not have to pay you royalties when you perform your record for promotional purposes.

15. **Merchandise.** The contract will typically state the percentage the label will pay you out of net (money leftover after expenses are paid) income from merchandise sales, if any. Typical expenses that will be paid before you are paid your royalties include manufacturing costs; costs of packaging, shipping, postage and insurance; and advertising and promotion expenses.

For example, the contract may state that the label will pay you 50% of net income from merchandise you sell at concerts and events after recoupment. Here is a breakdown of what this means:

T-shirt Retail price $20 (cost customer paid)

Costs $8 (manufacturing, packaging, etc.)

$12 (net income from sale)

$6 (amount you make per t-shirt. 50% of net income)

However, if you still owe the label money from costs that they initially paid for your album (recording, marketing, etc.), then the entire $6 will go toward them recouping their costs and you will earn $0 from the t-shirt sale until the label is repaid the amounts they initially spent on your album.

16. **Advances.** Pay special attention to any expenses that the label agrees to pay for. Always ask if something the label buys or pays for is "recoupable" or an "advance" (money you must pay back before they pay you). For example, many labels will require that you pay them back for the trademark search of your name, costs for independent publicists, website, out-of-pocket expenses for tour support, costs for promoters and marketing consultants, etc.

17. **Special Appearances.** Your contract may state that you must appear, subject to your reasonable availability, for any special appearances. Oftentimes, you *will not* be paid for such promotional services unless you negotiate otherwise. They may include a clause stating that they will reimburse you for pre-approved travel and living expenses but you usually have to ask for this.

18. **Your Image / Likeness.** Most record label contracts state that they are the only ones that can use your image or likeness during the contract term for promotion of your music (unless they give permission). They may also state that they can use your future artist names to promote albums in the future. Many agreements will state that no one else can use your likeness during the contract term for distributing, selling, advertising, or exploiting records without their approval. Some agreements allow the label to use your image and likeness forever while others can only use it until the contract ends.

19. **Exclusive.** While under contract, you typically cannot do any work that could keep you from being able to promptly perform your services for the label. Most contracts prohibit you from recording, manufacturing, distributing, selling, authorizing or permitting your performances to be recorded by anyone for any reason without the label approving it in writing.

You may also have to get the label's approval before performing or featuring on any other artist's song. If you make any records for motion pictures, television, radio, etc., you can usually only do it if the label signs a contract giving permission to the production company. Most contracts also require that you agree to only perform for the label or with their permission during the contract term.

Key Terms to Negotiate

Here are just a few of the key terms you can and negotiate to make sure you get the best deal possible:

1. **Retain ownership of your music (own rights to your masters)** Share with the label that you are not comfortable giving away all of the rights to your music (including songs you wrote before you signed with the label) as you are concerned that you may not be able to support yourself financially. You can then offer to give them a percentage of income from the songs during the time you are under contract with them.

2. **Remove the renewal options from the contract.** You can share that you want a chance to see how the arrangement works out first before committing to multiple terms with the label. Or, you can negotiate that renewals must be based on both parties (you and the label) agreeing to extend for an additional term. Make sure the contract requires that this agreement be in writing so that the label cannot later argue that you agreed to an extension when you did not.

3. **Keep 100% of your Merchandise.** Share that you need your merchandise income to be able to support yourself financially since the contract may not include any other guaranteed income (outside of advances that must be repaid).

4. **Advances must be approved by you in writing.** Request that the final budget, which lists any purchases the label plans to make on your behalf that are recoupable (you have to pay back), be submitted to you in writing and approved by you first. This makes sure that you do not end up owing the label a large amount of money that you cannot repay (many famous musicians and artists have had to file bankruptcy due to failing to negotiate these types of terms).

5. **Use of Your Image/Likeness.** Request that the label only be allowed to use your image and likeness while you are under contract with them. After your contract expires, the label should have to get your approval or negotiate a new deal with you in order to still be able to use your image and likeness to promote their brand.

Now that we have discussed recording artist agreements and the pros and cons of signing with a major label, let's talk about what it will take for you to earn a full time income from your music.

Chapter 6: How to Work Full Time in Music

It is not as difficult as it may seem to work full-time running your own music business. For many songwriters, producers, artists, and musicians, it may seem nearly impossible to create enough business for music to replace your full-time job. However, if you want to create a full-time income from your music business, all you need is a plan and the commitment to see it through.

Know How Much Money You Need

The first step in developing your plan is to know how much you need to make in order to support yourself full time. Then, you will need to track and manage the money that you earn to make sure it is going where you want it to go.

Here are some simple steps to creating your plan for financial freedom by first knowing how much money you need to make:

Step One:

How much do you need to earn each year to support yourself? $_____
(e.g., $35,000, $40,000, $50,000, etc.)

Do not write one million dollars. Instead, realistically estimate your monthly bills (rent or mortgage, car note, insurance, student loans, phone, food, etc.) and multiply this number by 12 to find out the minimum amount that you would need your music business to earn each year. Here is an example:

Monthly Bills:

Rent:	$800
Car:	$300
Insurance:	$200
Food:	$100
Savings:	$50
Cell Phone:	$50 +
	$1,500

$1,500 (Monthly Bills) x 12 (months) = $18,000 (minimum amount you need to make each year to support yourself)

Step Two:

Divide the number you listed in step one by 52. Since there are 52 weeks in a year, this new number will tell you how much you need to earn each week from your music business to be able to support yourself full-time.

$18,000 (yearly bills) / (divided by) 52 (weeks) = $346 per week

For example, if you need to earn $18,000 per year, you would need to bring in at least $346 each week in music income.

Step Three:

Commit yourself to focusing each week on looking for ways and opportunities to raise this amount. For example, if you need $346 each week in music income, you may earn $50 each week in music lessons, $150 from performing at a local venue, $46 from CD sales at your events and through your website, $50 from selling a song that you wrote to another artist, and $50.00 for doing a feature on a friend's song. You can also earn income from licensing as discussed earlier in this book.

Once you know how much money you need each week in order to work full-time for yourself, let's discuss some ways to manage and track the money you bring in order to make sure you are meeting your goals.

What is Money Management?

Money management is all about having a plan for your money. I have a personal adage that says: *"If you don't have a plan for your money, your money will have a plan for you."* This simply means that in order to be successful at running your own music business, it's not enough to make money. You then have to have a plan for what you want your money to do once you have it. Otherwise, it will do what it does best - disappear.

How to Manage Your Money

One of the best ways to manage your money is to have a system for tracking it. Tracking your money lets you know exactly how much money you're bringing in, tells you the things you're doing that make the most profit, and the things that may be causing you to lose money.

For example, does it ever feel like whenever you make money it seems to disappear so quickly? Money has a way of getting lost and ending up in places we don't want it to be if it is not intentionally guided and directed. Think about it. It seems like whenever get paid, a friend needs to borrow money, your favorite store is having a sale, plus your car breaks down and needs to be repaired.

Money management is all about having a plan for where you want your money to go and carrying out that plan as soon as you get money. This allows you to take care of current bills while constantly putting money aside for bigger goals. This "plan" is commonly referred to as a budget. But let's not get too ahead of ourselves. Instead, we'll start by discussing the second step to managing your money which is tracking the money that you make.

There are many ways to maintain your system for tracking and managing your money. You can buy software, download apps, or use financial management websites. Before you invest in one of these more advanced tools, let's at least learn some of the primary functions that these applications offer so you will understand the basics behind tracking and managing your money before you let technology take over for you.

Track the Money You Make

To begin, you will want to start by keeping a record of the money that you make. You want to organize your records based on where the money came from so that you know the things that you are doing that earn the most money as well as the things that you are doing that earn the least amount of money.

Example: At the end of each week, write down where the money you made from your music business came from:

$150   Fee for live performance
$50   T-shirt sales from after the show
$50   CD sales from after the show

This is important because the IRS is always comparing the money that you have in your bank account with the money that you say you made on your tax returns. The government wants to make sure that you're paying your fair share of taxes on the money that you earn. If they find out that you are not reporting all of your income, you could face severe penalties including possible jail time.

Tracking the money that you make also lets you know what you should spend more time doing. If it takes you one hour to give a music lesson and you make $40 – but it takes you one hour to play at a wedding and you make $300, you may want to focus on booking more weddings.

However, be sure to include *all* of the time that you spend and all of the expenses (bills) that you pay when you compare the business services you offer. For example, performing at a wedding may only take one hour but if you have to drive 30 minutes each way to get to downtown where most weddings are held, you're really only making $150 per hour. Here is how it works:

30 minutes (travel to wedding)
30 minutes (travel home from wedding)
<u>1 hour performance at wedding</u>
Total time: 2 hours

$300 (amount you're paid) divided by 2 hours (time spent) = **$150 per hour** (amount you're really making each hour you play at weddings

If playing at weddings actually takes you 2 hours driving back and forth, one hour to perform, one hour to mingle with the wedding party and get paid, plus 2 hours to rehearse and learn the specific songs, then you're really only making $50 per hour ($300 divided by 6 hours spent = $50 per hour).

In this case, focusing on getting more music students may require less effort and would be more profitable than weddings if you limited your lessons to 30 minutes.

Here is how it works:

30 minute lesson = $40
30 minute lesson = $40
$80 per hour giving music lessons

Hopefully, you can now see how tracking the money you make as well as tracking the time you spend can help you make better decisions when running your music business.

Track the Money You Spend

Now that you know how to track the money you make and the time you spend, you also need to track the money you spend. As a business owner, you can deduct (write off on your taxes) many of the expenses (bills) that you have when you are running your music business. Here are some common expenses that you can write off on your taxes, which may help lower the amount of taxes you have to pay on money you earn:

Example:

$12   Domain for Website
$200   T-shirt Inventory for Sale
$500   CD Inventory

$150   Promotional material for concerts

$700   Home Studio equipment

However, in order to legally be able to write off your expenses, you need to have proof that you actually spent the money that you say you did on things related to your business. You can do this by always asking for a receipt when you buy things for your business and saving them (or a digital copy) so that you can easily find them. Sometimes taking a photo of receipts with your camera phone and saving them is an easy way to keep track of them.

It's important to keep your business receipts because the I.R.S. has the legal authority to audit you (check your records). If you are ever audited, you will need to be able to prove that what you listed on your tax return was actually purchased and that it is a legitimate business expense. Otherwise, you may face severe penalties. You can visit www.IRS.gov to learn more about the criteria for business deductions to make sure that the items you write off on your taxes are recognized business expenses for I.R.S. purposes.

Track Money People Owe You

Now that you have tracked the money you have made and the money you have spent, you need to track any money that people owe you (referred to as "receivables" in business). I always recommend that my clients get their money up front whenever possible when running their businesses to avoid having people owe you money that they never pay back.

However, in the event that people do owe you money, it is important to keep records. You can also speak with an attorney about filing for a judgment against them or other legal collection methods to reclaim the funds that you are owed. In some cases, the law allows you to get title to their property or other equipment that they own if they have not repaid you. Be sure to speak with a lawyer for details.

Here is an example of how to track money that you may be owed:

Example:

Producer owes $150 for track
Artist owes $100 for studio rental
Music student owes $50 for lessons

Track the Money You Owe People

Now, it's time to track the money you owe other people. In business, we call this "accounts payable." Think of any regular bills you have for your music business (cell phone, internet, etc.). You will also want to list any outstanding debt such as credit card debt as well as personal loans from friends or family members. This list is important because it will allow you to understand exactly how much you need to make each month to be able to make your current payments on monthly bills as well as keep up with your payments on credit card bills and other debts. You'll want to track the total amount you owe, when the monthly payments are due, as well as how much you have to pay each month.

Example:

$1,000 Music Store Credit Card Purchase
Payments: $100 each month
Balance Owed: $900
Next Payment Due: Dec. 30th

Track Your Inventory

In addition to tracking money people owe you and money you owe, you need to keep records of the merchandise and products that you have on hand (called "inventory"). You will need to report your business inventory on your taxes. This will also help you keep track of items that you need to re-order, items that are selling the most, and items that are the most profitable.

Example:

July Inventory

5	Large T-shirts
15	Medium T-shirts
20	Small T-shirts
150	CDs (first album)
60	CDs (second album)

30   Band cell phone covers

You should review your inventory regularly and compare each month to see which items are selling the most, which activities or venues allow you to sell the most, and which items you may want to stop ordering due to lack of interest.

Hopefully, you can now see that working full time in your music business starts with knowing how much you need to make each week to meet your annual goals. Once you know how much you need, you can focus on making sure that you bring in that amount each week from your music business. Learning to consistently track the money you're bringing in, as well as how you're spending it, will help you make better decisions toward working full time in music.

Now that we have discussed how to work full time for yourself in music, let's dive into some key aspects of your business that you may want to monitor to help you know if your music business is growing enough to ultimately support you full time.

Chapter 7: How to Know if Your Business is Growing

Now that you are running your own music business, you'll find that there is always something to do. You can try to book more shows. You can interact with your fans via social media. You can spend time writing more music. There will always be something new competing for your time.

Truly successful businesses are able to determine which business activities are actually helping their business grow and they intentionally spend more time doing those things. You see, not everything you spend time on will result in growth for your business. And the more your business grows – the closer you'll be to working full time for yourself (if this is your goal).

So, how do you know which business activities will result in growing your business? You have to track what you are doing and how you are spending your time. We've already discussed how to track where your money is going so that you know how to direct your money toward the things that will make your business profitable. Now we'll learn how to track your time so that you can do more of the things that bring in business and less of the things that do not.

Music Business Numbers

This is where numbers come in. You need to track the numbers relating to the important aspects of your music business so that you can measure how effective or successful your efforts are. Instead of just spending your days doing things that you *think* are helping you grow your music business, you're going to start tracking these particular numbers so that you know for certain which activities are helping your music business grow and which ones are just taking up your time.

Here are just a few key numbers you can track regularly to help you determine if your music business is growing:

Artist/Band/Musician Numbers

1. How many people invited you to perform at events this month?

    - Write down the number of invitations you received this month.

    - Write down any specific actions you took that may have resulted in you receiving the invitation. (For example, maybe you sent out a newsletter or posted on Facebook that you are available to be booked).

- You should review this number regularly so that you know which marketing efforts are helping you grow your business.

- Please note that some marketing activities take time to produce a result. The goal here is to do your best to determine the relationship between certain things you are doing to promote your business – and you actually being hired.

* If you start seeing that you are receiving less invitations each month, then you need to stop and look at your business! This may mean that you need to do more to communicate with promoters that may want to hire you (e.g., meet them for lunch, call, etc.). You may need to communicate more with your fans to remind them that you are available to be booked (e.g., send a newsletter, Instagram posts, Facebook posts, twitter posts, host a contest, write a blog, etc.) Or, you may even need to evaluate your music and brand in comparison to other artists in your music category to make sure you are relevant and meeting the needs of your supporters.

2. **Of the people that hired you, how many were repeat customers?** The more repeat customers you have, the better. If no one ever

anchor clients

hires you a second time, send a survey or an e-mail to find out why.

3. **How did they hear about you?** Is there a particular person telling everyone about you? Be sure to send each person that refers someone to you a thank you card, take them out to lunch, or setup a referral program where they receive a gift card for every person that hires you that they referred to you. This will encourage more people to work for your business by spreading the word - which may result in more bookings.

4. **How many hired you after you quoted them?** If you are giving lots of quotes but no one ever hires you, send a follow up e-mail or survey to find out why. You may be priced too high, you may need to revise your services to meet the needs of your market (e.g., other bands play for 1 hour for a certain price while you only play for 30 minutes for the same price), or you may need to update your branding (website, social media profiles, etc.) to meet the needs of your market.

5. **What feedback did they leave on your survey?** If several people complain that your band arrived late or that you did not sign autographs afterward, be sure to at least consider modifying your business practices.

6. **How much money did you make?** Compare the money you earned at each event in comparison to your costs. For example, if you made $400, but you had to pay almost all of it to band members, it may be more profitable for you to book events where you can perform to a track and take home more pay yourself.

7. **How many albums did you sell at each event?** Make sure your display table is organized and features current branding (e.g., retractable banner, tablecloth with your logo, merchandise and albums). Make sure you are able to accept credit and debit cards. Visit these sites for payment devices you can connect to your cell phone:

    www.SquareUp.com
    www.Paypal.com

8. **How much merchandise did you sell? What was most popular?** If your gear is not selling, ask for honest feedback from supporters. Consider having new designs created. Send the designs to your fans before you spend money printing them and let your fans vote on their favorites to let you know which designs will be a hit.

Songwriter/Producer Numbers

1. **How many people asked you to write a song or make a beat/music this month?** This number should grow the longer you are in

business. If not, you may want to considering taking classes to improve your songwriting techniques as well as spending more time marketing your services to get the word out.

2. **How many of them have hired you before?** You want to see repeat clients. If not, you may want to send a survey to past clients to ask if there is anything you can do to improve your service to earn their business again.

3. **How did they hear about you?** You may want to send a thank you card or offer incentives (free gift cards, etc.) to people that refer business to you often.

4. **How many hired you after you quoted them?**

If you find that all of the people that you have been contacting and giving quotes to are no longer hiring you, then it may be a good time for you to take a look at your prices to make sure that you are not too expensive.

You can also send a survey (www.SurveyMonkey.com) to find out if there is another reason that the individuals did not hire you. You would be amazed at the honest feedback that people will give you when you ask.

However, never make a decision solely based on feedback. You have to be able to live with yourself and the decisions that you make so don't compromise your values or dramatically change your entire identify just because of one person's survey. However, if you find yourself noticing trends within your music business, you may want to at least look into them. Perhaps it is time for you to get better quality production, get professional photos, hire an image consultant, get a more professional website, or hire a professional songwriter as opposed to attempting to do it all yourself.

5. **What feedback did they leave on your survey?** Look for patterns. If one person made a particular comment, it may just be an aberration. If multiple people reference the same thing about your business, it may be worth making an adjustment or at least looking into.

6. **How much money did you make?** You want to see growth but not just growth in the amount of money you are bringing in, but the amount of money you have leftover after all of the bills are paid.

7. **Are there any trends among the buyers?** If you notice that country music artists always buy your music, then you may want to make more deliberate efforts to reach that market.

Record Label Numbers

1. **How many artists does your label currently have on its roster?** If a large percentage of your artists choose not to renew their contracts, be sure to send them an exit survey to find out why.

2. **When was the last time each artist released an album?** Record labels vary with their theories regarding how often you should release albums. You just want to make sure that your artists are not waiting on you but that the label is actively finalizing projects so that they can be released to the public for sale.

3. **How long did it take you to produce each album?** Your goal is to have a quality yet timely process. Work to decrease aspects of the process that waste time in order to increase your productivity.

4. **How much did each album cost?** It may be time to contact your vendors to renegotiate rates for discounts based on the volume of business you give them or the length of time you've worked with them. It may also be helpful to shop around for quotes from their competition to help you negotiate.

5. **How many units did you sell?** You should see growth here. Pay attention to the specific venues where your label's music sells the most and focus more of your efforts on those platforms.

6. **How many shows have you booked for your artists?** If your artists are not regularly performing, you may need to hire a new booking agent, get new branding for the artists and label (new photographs, website, etc.) and begin building and reestablishing relationships with promoters.

7. **How many promotions have you booked for your artists?** Your goal is to increase your artists' exposure to help them sell more albums. You may need to consider hiring a new public relations agent and other team members to help book more promotions.

8. **How much revenue is the label making from royalties?** Make sure that all song catalogs are updated with their respective performance rights organizations to make sure you are receiving all of the royalties you are entitled to receive.

9. **Has your distribution increased or decreased in the past year?** Make sure you are increasing your presence based on the goals of your specific record label.

These are just a few examples of some of the factors that you may want to track in order to grow your music business. Again, these numbers are not all-inclusive and may vary among music businesses. Not all of them will apply to your music business and some that apply may not be listed. Instead, these numbers are just a starting point to help you begin to examine the business activities of your music business and track them to see if they are helping you grow.

Now that you are keeping up with the important numbers of your business in order to know if you are growing, it's time to learn how to know if your music business is profitable.

Chapter 8: How to Know if Your Business Is Profitable

A lot of people start music businesses. If you truly want to work for your music business full-time, it is not enough to have money coming in. You need to know at all times if your music business is "profitable" or earning a profit. To keep things simple, we will define "profit" as having money left over after you pay the bills of your music business.

If you are making money, but never have anything left over after paying the bills of the business, you may not have a business. You may have simply created a "bill" for yourself. A business should add money to your bank account - not simply take money away. Of course, it sometimes takes time for a business to become profitable. However, there are key indicators you can use to make sure that you are always moving closer toward being profitable – not further away.

What are Financial Statements

Every day, you are spending money and making money while running your business. Instead of having to spend hours pouring over hundreds or thousands of individual transactions (purchases and deposits) on the bank statements of your business account and doing the math to reach conclusions, businesses generate financial statements.

Financial statements are scorecards that let you view the health of a business by looking at a summary of its transactions or activities on a few pages. They are far less cumbersome than having to review hundreds of receipts and pages of bank statements. Financial statements are generated using a commonly accepted set of accounting principles or rules that allow business owners, managers, banks, and investors to compare businesses from different industries in a universal way. Financial statements are similar to sheet music for musicians. They allow people that are unfamiliar with a song, or in this case your business, to read the sheet music (financial statements) and immediately understand the music (the health of your business).

Why Financial Statements Are Important

Even though you are keeping your own records and tracking numbers for your music business, it may be a good idea to generate financial statements on a regular basis.

Financial statements can help your music business in the following ways:

1. **Know the health of your business.** Financial statements allow you to easily track many of the numbers we discussed to know if your business is healthy and growing.

2. **Know if your business is profitable.** Financial statements will allow you to see all of your expenses and your income on one page (typically). This will let you know immediately if you are making money or losing money in your business. For example, you will be able to see if the income from your shows, merchandise, and album sales is increasing. You can also tell if you're spending too much on studio time, equipment, or other costs.

3. **Allows Others to Understand Your Business.** In the future, you may decide that you would like to bring on investors or a business partner. You may even need to apply for a business loan or decide to sell your business and use the money you make to do something else. In each of these scenarios, you will likely need to have financial statements prepared for your business so that the other parties (investors, business partners, lenders, prospective buyers) can assess the health of your business.

4 Types of Financial Statements

There are four (4) primary types of financial statements: Income Statement (also known as the Profit & Loss Statement), Balance Sheet, Statement of Cash Flows, and Statement of Owner's Equity. It would take an entire book to discuss how powerful each of these financial statements are and explain all of the ways that they can benefit your music business. However, here is a brief overview of each statement:

1. **Income Statement / Profit & Loss Statement (P&L)** – On the most basic level, the Income Statement tells you how much money you made and the bills you had during a certain period of time. In order to make money in business, you will need to have money leftover after you pay all of your bills. This is a basic definition of "profit". The P&L lets you see the "bottom line" or your profit or loss after everything was paid during a specific time period (month, quarter, year, etc.) Here are just a few things an income statement will tell you about your business:

    - How well is your business performing
    - Is your business profitable (making money after the bills are paid)?
    - Are you over budget or paying too much in some areas?

2. **Balance Sheet** – The Balance Sheet lets you see your assets (things you own), your liabilities (what you owe others), and owner's equity (what the business owes the owners) at any given moment in your business. Examples of assets would be cash in your bank account, musical equipment your business owns, and accounts receivable (money other people owe you). Examples of liabilities

would be credit card debt, loans, and wages owed to employees. Owner's equity is the money your business owes the owners. Here are just a few of the things a balance sheet will let you know about your business:

- If you need more cash reserves (money saved)
- If you can handle more debt
- If you can handle growing or expanding
- Do you need to be more aggressive with collecting money owed to you?

3. **Statement of Cash Flows** – To put it simply, a Statement of Cash Flows tells you where your money is coming from and how it is being spent during a period of time. Some businesses are profitable but go out of business because they did not have enough "cash on hand" to pay their bills. This can happen if the timing of when your bills are due and when you get paid are not aligned. Your Statement of Cash Flows can help you see if this is or will be a problem and correct it in advance. Here are a few things you can learn about your business from reviewing your Statement of Cash Flows.

- How much are you bringing in from sales and day-to-day business operations?
- How much money did you use to pay owners?

- How much money did you use to buy equipment or other assets?
- How much money did you borrow?
- Are you bringing in enough cash to pay your bills?

4. **Statement of Owner's Equity** – The Statement of Owner's Equity shows the changes that were made to the owner's capital account in the business. Here is how it works. As the owner of a business, you own a stake in the business. This is known as having "equity" or ownership in the business. If you are a 100% owner (you do not have any business partners), then you own a 100% equity stake in the business.

   As an owner, you will typically contribute a certain amount of money to the business (capital contribution) to start operations. This amount is placed in your capital account. For example, if you as the owner initially put $1,000 into your business to get it started, then your capital account would show your balance as $1,000. As you add more capital to the business or make withdrawals, the Statement of Owner's Equity shows the changes to your capital account. Here are just a few of the things you can learn from reviewing the Statement of Owner's Equity for your business:

   - How much you have put into the business
   - How much you have taken out of the business

- How much you would receive out of the proceeds of a sale of the business

How to Create Financial Statements

Again, financial statements are a powerful tool for managing the performance of your music business. Here are a few ways that you can create financial statements to increase the effectiveness of your business operations:

1. **Do it Yourself.** You can buy software or an app for your cell phone or tablet or you can use a cloud-based financial management website to manage your money and create financial statements. You can also create them using Microsoft Excel templates. Although it may take you some time to understand everything when you first start, taking the time to learn how to read and understand these financial statements will make you a more savvy business owner and will help you communicate with others about your music business.

    Consider visiting **Lynda.com** for online classes and tutorials regarding understanding and creating financial statements.

2. **Hire a Bookkeeper or Accountant.** Later in the book, we will discuss how you can hire a bookkeeper or accountant to prepare financial statements for you.

Keep in mind, it's never too late to begin using these powerful financial tools as you run your music business. Now that we have learned ways to gauge the performance and profitability of your music business, let's talk about budgets and how to make sure you are positioned to reach your financial goals.

Chapter 9: How to Achieve Your Financial Goals

WHAT IS A BUDGET?

My definition of a budget is simply "having a plan for your money". As I've stated earlier in the book, *"if you do not have a plan for your money, your money will have a plan for you."* This means that if you do not take the initiative to plan and decide how you want to spend your money before you even earn it, when you do receive it, unexpected bills will come up and you'll end up spending your money on things you never expected to spend it on.

How Budgets Help Grow Your Business

Let me give you a real life example. Let's say you are a music producer and you get hired to produce a track for a new artist. As soon as you are paid by your client, you will immediately have a myriad of choices and options as far as how you can use your money. You can reinvest in new equipment, you can reinvest in a new wardrobe, you can buy additional studio time, you can hire help, or you can just spend the extra money hanging out.

However, not all options will actually help you to grow your music business. You should focus on buying things that will directly result in more clients or sales for your music business. How do you know what those things are? You should ask yourself *"If I buy this, will this directly result in more business?"* You should then list your options and how they would impact your business:

- **Buy new equipment** – This appears to be the obvious choice. If you buy fancier equipment, you'll get more clients. Right? Not always. You could end up spending all of your money on brand new studio equipment and still not have any new clients. This isn't always the case. If you have been turning away clients that were requesting this new equipment and were willing to pay enough to use it to cover the expense of the equipment plus leave you with a profit, then it may be a good investment. Otherwise, I would recommend realizing that the equipment you have is just fine and figure out a way to make it work so that you can use your limited funds toward investing in things that will grow your business.

- **Buy a new wardrobe** – Same analysis as above. There are times when a new wardrobe will help grow your business. But starting out, you'll want to be a bargain shopper (buy fashionable items for less – if you don't know how to do this, ask your most fashionable friend to go shopping with you). You can then spend your funds on things that will grow your business.

- **Hire help** – Now this may be a good option. What about spending $10/hour to find someone to call all of the artists you promised you would get back to on social media that asked about your production services? Or, hire a successful producer as a consultant to tell you how they run their business so that you can get more clients? Once you've done this, perhaps hiring a second producer to work for your business to allow you to be able to handle more clients since you've been recently having to turn people away may be a good option.

- **Marketing** – Find where your clients are and spend money reaching them where they are. If most of your clients are indie artists that perform at a certain venue, talk to the owner about becoming a sponsor so that you'll have an opportunity to showcase your work and connect one-on-one with your target market. If a certain website attracts your target client, consider buying an ad or asking to write as a guest blogger to get more exposure. This may take some work but find out where your clients are coming from and do more of what has worked in the past.

- **Invest in Yourself** – Buying books on business, finance, marketing, taking online classes, hiring a successful person (consultant) to teach you how they built their company are also great ways to reinvest your funds in order to grow your business.

Once you know the things that will help you grow your business, list them in your budget and use your budget as a financial roadmap. As soon as you get paid, look at your budget and spend the money exactly as you outlined it in your budget. Of course there are always emergencies, but try your best to follow it.

How to Create a Budget

Now it's time to create your budget. Creating a budget (a plan for your money) will involve two things: (1) you will need to list the money that you expect to receive; and (2) you will need to write a plan for how you want to spend that money. It's that simple!

You will list all the ways that you expect to receive money in the "income" category. You will then list how you want that money to be spent in the "expenses" category. Here is an example:

Best Band, LLC Budget
February 20__(Year)

<u>Income (Money You Will Receive)</u>
1. Album Sales $100

streaming Royalties

2. College Campus Performance $200

3. Merchandise Sales (T-shirts) $50

4. Flat Fee for Songs Sold $150

TOTAL: $500

Expenses (Where the Money Should Go)

1. Charity / Tithes $50

2. Flyers for Street Team $100

3. Hire Student as Booking Agent for 10 hours $100

4. Business Reserves / Savings $250

TOTAL: $500

As you make more money, you can set rules for where you want the money to go in order to keep your business growing. For example, 10% will always go to charity, 50% will be saved as business reserves, 40% will be reinvested in the business for growth (e.g., hiring help, producing new albums, marketing, etc.)

Example: Justin makes $400 over the weekend from performing. Based on the rules he set, he knows to pay $40 (10%) to his church to support their community food pantry for the homeless, $200 (50%) in his business savings [checking] account, $160 (40%) will be reinvested in the business for growth (he will use $60 toward a marketing fund to have a new website built and $100 to hire his responsible cousin to make phone calls to promoters and venues to help him book more events.

The Importance of Controlling Expenses.

Smart business owners budget their money in order to manage it and achieve their financial goals. However, you want to make sure that you are holding onto some of the money you make and not just spending it all. This is how you grow your music business. You have to learn to spend less than you make. It is much easier to keep the money that you already have than it is to earn new money. This means you will need to monitor your spending very carefully.

Business owners know that the only way to actually make a profit, or have money leftover after paying the bills, is to monitor how many bills they have. The less bills you have each month, the more money you make as "profit." This is the money you can use to (1) save and earn interest and (2) reinvest in your business (spend it on things that will make you even more money).

Controlling your expenses means thinking like a business owner – not an employee. Employees often think about spending company money to achieve a result. Smart businesses owners think about ways to (1) bring in more income; (2) reduce current expenses; and (3) reinvest their income in things that will make them more money in order to achieve a result. Here is an example of how it works:

Example: After paying all of her bills, Lisa has $500 left from her music business. She decides to save $200 in an account that she never touches that earns interest. Her goal is for the money in this account to grow to be worth $10,000 so that she can use the interest the money earns to pay some of her monthly bills. She spends the other $300 on hiring a college student to be her booking agent. She pays the student $10 an hour to make calls to promoters and conferences to book her for more shows. The $300 she spent on her booking agent has turned into over $1,000 in new booking fees for performances (which is a 233% return on investment!)

Again, the goal is to use a budget to make sure the money you make is working hard for you by paying your bills plus leaving you with extra leftover to save for the future (business reserves) and reinvest in things that will help you grow your current business. You will accomplish much more by making it a regular practice to take a look at your expenses and control the amount of purchases you make to keep your expenses from getting out of control.

Now that you understand how to create a budget and control your expenses to help you meet your financial goals for your music business, let's discuss the importance of managing debt and credit.

Chapter 10: Managing Debt & Credit

Another important principle that will help you as you are managing your money is learning how to responsibly manage debt and credit. Many people have their own opinions about debt. Some people strongly believe that debt is bad and you should pay cash for everything and avoid it at all costs. Some people rely on debt for everything. They have multiple consumer credit cards, regularly buy things they cannot afford and live paycheck to paycheck. Others strategically use credit cards for rewards points and responsibly pay them off at the end of the month to avoid interest charges. You get to decide the best way to manage debt for yourself. However, here are a few guidelines that may help you manage debt responsibly:

Ways to Manage Debt Responsibly

1. **Pay cash when possible.** Try your best to spend money that you have instead of living off of credit cards or debt when possible. This means that if you do not have enough cash in your bank

account to pay for something, the goal is to wait and save up until you can afford it.

An easy way to have the discipline (self-control) to do this is to remind yourself of the difference between things we "want" and things that we "need." Our economy is largely supported by companies spending millions of dollars each year to convince you that you "need" things that are actually something that you just "want." Always remind yourself that artists, musicians, bands, and producers many years ago were able to accomplish the same things (spreading the word, producing quality music, etc.) for their music businesses without many of the luxuries that companies will try and convince you that you "need." If you can have the discipline to keep your "wants" in perspective, you'll find yourself always having money leftover to save and reinvest.

2. **Be creative.** If you find that you truly "need" something for your business but you still do not have enough cash to pay for it, you can try and use one of these creative – yet legal - means to get things that you need:

- Barter – this is when someone gives you a service or good in exchange for you giving them another service or good. For example, someone could let you use their home studio for an hour in exchange for you agreeing to let them borrow your guitar for an upcoming performance.

- Buy used – check out online stores such as Amazon, Ebay or Craig's List to find deals on used items in good condition.
- Ask for open-box sales – If you're shopping at a retail store, ask if they will sell the display item at a discount or if they have any open box or refurbished items.
- Negotiate – If there is a service you want to hire someone for that is more than what you can afford, try to negotiate. "That amount is really outside of my budget. Is there any way you would do it for [insert your own amount]?"

3. **Use "Interest Free" Promotions.** You can also take advantage of "interest free" offers that certain stores have when you are making large purchases. For example, certain music stores will allow you to have 12 months without paying any interest if you make a purchase using their store credit card. This does not mean that you do not have to make any payments for a year. Instead, this just means you will only have to make the monthly minimum payment (typically $25 or $30 per month) by the deadline each month and they will not charge interest.

The key to taking advantage of interest free special financing promotions as a means of paying for your music equipment is to have the discipline to pay more than the minimum balance each month so that you can have the entire debt paid off before they start charging you interest.

Make sure you specifically call the customer service department and have them review all of the terms of the credit card, the due dates for payments and rules for charging interest so that you can avoid any finance charges. If you know that you will not have regular and reliable income to make the payments and pay off the balance before the end of the interest free promotion, you may want to avoid this option.

4. **Use Good Debt.** If you must use debt, make sure it is "good debt." Good debt is debt that will make you more money. For example, using a credit card to buy clothes may only result in you having a new "bill" to repay. However, using debt in the form of a small business loan to lease a building that you will use as a studio and make $1,500 profit (after paying the monthly loan payment) is good debt. The fact that you are using the bank's money to make more money for yourself is referred to as "leverage."

5. **Keep Good Records.** In the event that you do have loans or credit card debt that you need to pay, you need to make sure that you keep good records so that they cannot say that you owe them more than you do or claim that you never paid them when you did. Keeping track will also help you make sure that you make all of your necessary payments each month to avoid late fees or interest charges.

10 Ways to Improve Your Credit Score

If you decide to use credit, you will want to make sure you take certain steps to protect and improve your credit score. Your credit score is the number that lenders will use to evaluate your creditworthiness, or your reliability when it comes to paying back money you borrow. Here are just a few ways to make sure you're protecting your credit score:

1. **Review Your Score** – Make sure you take advantage of the opportunity to pull a free credit report each year from each of the three major credit bureaus: Transunion, Experian and Equifax. You can visit www.AnnualCreditReport.com to get the report. You don't have to pull all three at the same time. Instead, pull one every 4 months from a different bureau so that you can monitor your credit activity throughout the year. Keep in mind that the report on your activity is free but you may have to pay a separate fee if you want the actual score.

2. **File a dispute** - When you get your report, you'll want to look to see if anything is wrong or inaccurate. Look for any (1) any bills or purchases that you did not authorize (which could be signs that someone has stolen your identity); (2) accounts that are paid off that are still showing a balance owed; or (3) open accounts that you have that are showing the wrong balance. If you find a mistake or

error on your credit report, call the credit bureau and request to dispute the account. They will document it in your file. You may also need to call your bank to have them issue a new credit or debit card and report the fraudulent purchase if in fact your identity has been stolen.

3. **Settle your debts** – If you have legitimate unpaid accounts, consider reaching out to the creditor to settle the debt. Oftentimes, debt collectors will settle a debt (accept less than the amount owed) for pennies on the dollar. This means that if you owe a bill collector $500, they may be willing to accept $200 paid at one time to settle it. They may also be willing to work out a payment plan for the $200. Here are a few things to keep in mind:

- Anything you say to them may be used against you. Be mindful of the personal information that you share.
- Make sure the debt collector you call actually provides you with proof that they own the debt so that you are not paying someone that is not the true owner. Sometimes debts get sold to several different debt collectors so you'll want to get a copy of the actual documentation that shows that they own the debt.
- Have the debt collector sign a written release. A release means that they are releasing you from any other claims that they have against you. You'll also want an indemnification clause that says they will pay to defend you in court if in fact someone

else claims that the debt is still owed. You can have an attorney draft a Release rather inexpensively.

4. **Pay your bills on time** – For your credit accounts that are active, make sure you pay your bills on time. Call the companies that you have consumer credit cards and debt and ask about the payment windows. It is possible to pay a bill "too early." If you pay before the new bill is issued, the company will sometimes apply your payment to the previous month instead of the next month. Make sure you know the timelines so that your payments arrive on time.

5. **Don't Use All of Your Credit** – Aim to use less than 30% (10% is best) of your available credit. For example, if the local music store gives you $5,000 in credit, then try to use no more than $1,500 or less. If you have a month where you have to make a big purchase ($3,000 on a $5,000 available credit card) then pay your bill twice that month - even if you're planning to pay it all off before the end of the month – so that it does not negatively affect your credit score.

6. **Make sure credit limits are accurate** – You want to make sure that the credit limits listed on your credit report are not lower than they are in reality. Lower limits will make it look like you're using a higher percentage of your available credit which hurts your score. Have this adjusted.

7. **Pay them off** – Try your best to pay off the balance of your card before the end of the month so that you are not charged interest. If you must pay it over the course of several months, make sure you always pay more than the minimum or you may be stuck paying for a $300 purchase for several years.

8. **Don't open too many accounts** - Try not to open too many credit accounts as this may negatively affect your credit score.

9. **Don't close accounts.** Instead of closing old accounts, you can sometimes use them for a smaller monthly bill that you can pay off each month (e.g., internet bill). Older accounts show that you have history which may be good for your overall credit score.

10. **Build credit** – If your credit score is low, you can work to rebuild it. Try getting a small personal loan or secure loan from your bank. Borrow the money. Don't spend it. Pay it right back the next month. Repeat this process and it may help you rebuild your credit.

Overall, if you manage debt and credit responsibly, you can continue to position yourself and your business for future growth. Now that we've talked about debt and credit, let's discuss how you can run your business like a business.

Chapter 11: How to Run Your Business

How You Run Your Business Matters

Throughout the book, we have learned how to make more money for your music business through licensing, how to negotiate better deals for you and your team through industry contracts, and how to increase your "bottom line" or profit with financial management strategies.

However, even if you understand all of those concepts, it is still important that you run your business like a business. This means that your business operations (the way you do business) must be done in such a way that the I.R.S. is convinced that you are running a business – instead of just doing music as a "hobby". A hobby is something that you do for fun – not necessarily to make a profit. The best way for me to illustrate this important principle is through an example.

Example: Corey starts a music business selling music that he makes using his studio software in his apartment. However, his day job is stressful and he never seems to have any time to grow his music business.

One day, his friend Jennifer tells him that owning a business has "perks" and he can get special tax breaks if he buys things for his music business.

Corey uses the tax software he bought from a grocery store and deducts different items he bought during the year. A few months after filing his taxes, Corey receives a notice from the I.R.S. that he is being audited. The I.R.S. asked him a number of specific questions and concluded that he did not have a business but instead had a hobby. The I.R.S. said that he was not legally able to take advantage of any of the tax benefits related to running a business and penalized him for the information he put on his tax returns.

10 Ways to Avoid IRS Trouble

The goal is for you to avoid being in the same position that Corey found himself in as it pertained to his music "hobby." Here are some things that you can do to make sure that you are running your music company like a real business and not a hobby:

1. **Schedule Time** - Set a specific time every day or every week that you will work on your business. For example, your "office hours" can be from 6 pm to 8 pm.

2. **Business Journal** - Keep a business journal and write down what you accomplished each day for your music business during your office hours.

Example: "Monday, December 1, I called and sent emails to people I met in the music store that said they might be interested in hiring me to perform."

3. **Make a Profit.** Make sure that you spend enough time within your business to show that you are actually trying to make a profit. For example, if making your album costs you $6.00, then you may want to sell it for $10 so that you earn a $4.00 profit per album ($10 - $6 = $4). Once you have a set "profit margin" (the difference between the sale price and the cost to make it), you can increase your profit by selling your albums regularly (e.g., after your shows, on your website, asking friends and family, etc.)

4. **Set Goals** - Set monthly sales goals to sell a certain number of albums, merchandise, or book a specific number of shows so that you are making a reasonable profit each month.

5. **Limit Freebies** - Although it is a trend in the music industry for artists to give music away for free to get fans and gain exposure, if you are not selling any of your music, this may present problems for you when it comes to the I.R.S.

6. **Let the Business Pay Bills.** There is nothing wrong with having multiple streams of income, or making money from different jobs and activities. However, the I.R.S. wants to see that you depend on the income from your business activities.

Example: For every $20.00 in profit that you make from selling merchandise, you can set aside $10.00 to go toward paying yourself. You can then use that income to pay a portion of your rent every month.

7. **Work to Improve Your Business.** Let's talk about business losses. The I.R.S. understands that businesses may have a slow period of time where they are not making a profit. However, the I.R.S. wants to see that you have taken a close look at your operations (activities) and changed in an effort to improve your profitability. For example, if you perform for free at local events and you never seem to be able to sell any CDs after your events, the I.R.S. would want to see that you have changed your actions by perhaps requesting that the event pay you a minimum amount to perform such as $100 so that you can make a profit.

8. **Invest in your Business Education.** It is important that you keep learning in order to grow your business. For example, invest in yourself and your development as a business owner. Buy books and resources to help you learn more about the music industry and running a business. The I.R.S. will look at the steps you have taken to learn how to run a successful business to determine how serious you are about your business.

9. **Meet with Advisors.** The I.R.S. will want to see that you have surrounded yourself with others that are more knowledgeable in the music industry that can help you grow and succeed. Attend music workshops and conferences in your area. Network with other producers, songwriters, artists, and labels on social media and develop relationships. Meet regularly with your lawyer, accountant, and financial advisor for strategic direction and guidance.

10. **Grow Your Business Assets.** The I.R.S. may also look at the assets of the business to see if they can be used to make a profit in the future. Building a catalog of songs, having music available for purchase, and having merchandise are all ways to show that you own assets that can be expected to have value in the market. This is another helpful way to show that your business is in fact a business and not just a hobby.

How to Hold Business Meetings

In my first book, "*Start Your Music Business*", we discussed the different types of business entities that you can form. We also discussed the fact that some types of businesses require you to use "corporate formalities." Corporate formalities means that you may have to hold a certain number of business meetings each year, write down the decisions that were voted upon in meeting minutes (notes), and write resolutions or statements showing the support of the owners for decisions made within the business.

Although businesses like LLCs do not require corporate formalities, I strongly recommend that you still treat your business like a business. Even if you do not have any investors, shareholders, business partners or even employees, I recommend that you still run your business as if you have to be accountable to someone.

This means you run your business as if you will have to give a report to someone about (1) how you have been spending your time; (2) the progress that has been made (or lack thereof); (3) and your strategies for improvement moving forward. You can accomplish this by holding regular business meetings for your music business.

You can have a weekly meeting, a monthly meeting, a quarterly meeting (a meeting held four times a year) or even meet once a year. However, I recommend setting aside a few hours in your schedule to review the operations of your music business at least four times a year. This means that you will sit down and look at the numbers you've tracked, the financial statements you've created, and your past client surveys since your last meeting. Here are a few factors to reflect upon during your business meeting:

1. **Income.** How much income have you made during those past four months? Was it more or less than the previous four months? What did you do differently?

2. **Expenses.** How much did you spend for the past four months? Are there ways you can further reduce your expenses? Can you borrow or rent items to avoid having to make so many purchases? Can you just use the equipment that you have until you reach a certain financial goal then reward yourself with a new purchase?

3. **Services.** What were your most popular services? What were your least popular services? How profitable are they? What strategies can you use to get more customers?

4. **Customers.** How many new clients/customers did you have? Was it more or less than the previous four months? How did they find you? What marketing strategies did you use for the past four months? Are there any trends with the types of people that are hiring you that you can use to target and find more people like them? What are the typical amounts they are willing to pay? What are your surveys saying?

5. **Operations.** How are you spending your time? What is working? What is not working? What are ways you can grow?

6. **Team.** Who is on your team? What skills do they have? What are things you do not know or understand? Who can you hire that has skills that you do not have to help you grow your business?

For example, during your business meeting, you may see that less people have been requesting you to perform. You may also notice that more people are buying your songs or hiring you for music lessons. As you are looking at your numbers, try to identify trends or things that keep occurring within your business so that you know what works and what does not work.

Sometimes there are certain things that you will do for your business that take time for you to see the benefit. For example, if you recently started a mailing list and you are not seeing immediate results, this does not mean that it is not working altogether. Instead, you may just need to be patient and give it more time. However, having a monthly meeting to evaluate your business will allow you to catch problems earlier and make strategic changes so that you can continue to grow.

Example: The first Saturday of each month, Alice invites her band to her apartment to talk about their music business. She serves snacks while they review the numbers from the previous month. They look at how many places booked them to perform, how much they made from each booking, and feedback the places gave them afterward on their survey.

From the numbers, they decide that (1) more weddings are hiring them; (2) they are able to charge the most when they play for the ceremony and reception; and (3) the parents that hire them prefer that they dress up for the events. They decide to spend time reaching out to wedding planners. They will introduce their band, send them a sample of their music and ask them to refer their brides. In exchange, they'll pay the wedding planners $25 for each bride that they refer that books them for a wedding.

Developing a Strategic Plan for your Business

Once you've held your business meeting, the next thing you need to do is develop a plan to use the information you have learned about your business. This is called strategic planning. Many people talk about problems or issues within their business, but few people take the time to actually set goals and write a plan to make changes. A strategic plan outlines the goals you have set based on your business meeting and a plan of action to achieve those goals. However, to be effective, a strategic plan should include the following:

1. **Where You Are** – Look at yourself and honestly write down where your music business is currently. In your mind, you may think you are a multi-platinum pop artist. In reality, you may be an up and coming artist that is trying to develop into a pop artist. You may really be an okay performer or a mediocre songwriter. Be honest so

that you know how you need to grow. If this is tough, ask some folks that you trust and feel they would be honest with you regarding the current state of your music business.

2. **Where You Want to Be** – What is your goal? Do you want to be a full-time songwriter? A producer with steady business. A record label with signed artists making money for you. An independent artist making enough to support yourself and pay the bills with album sales, merchandise, and performances. A signed artist with a major record label. Write specifically where you want your music business to be.

3. **How you will get there** – This may be the most important step and is often the step that successful music businesses focus on. This is your plan of action.

5 Steps to a Powerful Plan of Action

Here are a few tips to writing a plan of action that will help you take your music business to the next level.

1. **Set Measurable Goals** – Write goals that you can measure. For example:

"I will call 10 agents each week to see if they will work with me in order to help me book more shows."

This is a goal you can measure because at the end of the week, you can check to see if you actually made all 10 calls.

2. **Write Specific Steps** – Next, you will need to break down the goal into specific steps that need to take place to make the goal happen. For example:

   First, I will read a few books and blogs on how to find a good agent.
   Next, I will search for "music agents in Chicago" and get a list of agents to contact.
   Lastly, I will write a script outlining what I need to say when I call the agents based on the information I learn during my research.

3. **Delegate.** You don't have to do it all. Find friends or contacts that believe in you and want to help. Assign one person to be responsible for doing each step. They can work with others but there needs to be one person that is responsible otherwise the entire group will just blame each other and things may not get done.

4. **Progress Reports.** Your team members should give regular (e.g., weekly) reports to the entire team to hold themselves accountable and make sure they are making progress.

5. **Deadlines.** Set a deadline for when each step should be done. Otherwise, you may show up at your next meeting and find that the same steps need to be taken since no one did them.

6. **Follow-up.** At the end of each meeting, you should have everyone open their calendars in order to schedule the next follow-up meeting. You'll also want to go over everyone's responsibilities and let them know that you will be discussing them at the next meeting in order to make sure that everyone does their part.

7. **Celebrate.** Sometimes we feel that the only accomplishments are "big" accomplishments. You may feel that you don't deserve to celebrate until you have a song playing on the radio, or you sell 100,000 units, or you win a Grammy. Life is short. We can set goals but we're not promised to accomplish them. That is why it's important to celebrate each milestone and every accomplishment – big or small. It will increase morale and allow you to enjoy every moment of your journey. Anyone that knows me personally knows that I believe in celebrating accomplishments (big and small) along the way – and I enjoy celebrating with others!

Example: Alice writes the following plan of action for her band:

<u>Plan of Action</u>
Goal: Book 5 more weddings each month
Steps:

(1) Make a list of all of the wedding planners in the city. (2) Call 10 wedding planners a day and offer them $25 for every wedding they refer to the band that books them.

Responsible Party: Alice will make the list. Clarence will make the calls.

Due Date: The list should be ready for Clarence by the end of the week. Clarence should have the calls completed by the end of the month.

Follow-up: Clarence will e-mail a weekly report to the band sharing the results of his calls. The band will meet next month at Alice's apartment to review the results and adjust the plan if needed.

Now that you know how to hold a business meeting, write a strategic plan, and prepare a plan of action for your business, let's discuss the actual records you'll need to keep your business in compliance.

Chapter 12: Business Recordkeeping

Now that you're running your own music business, your actions no longer affect just you. As a business owner, you're accountable to the government (e. g., state and federal government), the people that work with you (your band members, producer, manager, record label, etc.), people that you hire (e. g., studios, vendors, songwriters, graphic designers, photographers, videographers) as well as the people that support you (your fans, your family, friends, co-workers, etc.).

This means that you need to make sure that you keep proper financial records, business records, and proper tax records to remain in compliance with the law. Here are a few of the main records that you need to keep in a safe place in order to protect yourself as well as your business:

Financial Records

1. **Business bank account statements.** Keeping your bank account statements are important because your bookkeeper may need them

when preparing your financials. You may also need them in order to get a business loan, if you ever want to bring on a business partner, or if you decide to sell your business in the future. Here are a few guidelines for managing your business bank account:

- Have a separate bank account for your music business.
- Do not buy personal items using your business account. This is called co-mingling. Instead, write yourself a salary check from your business account (or follow the rules your accountant outlines depending on the business entity you have chosen), deposit it into your personal account and then pay the personal bill out of your personal bank account.
- Check your bank statements (called "reconciling") each month to make sure the balances are correct and that you have not been charged for bank fees or fees you did not approve.

2. **Business Bank Account Deposit Slips.** Particularly if you accept cash, you should make copies or download your deposit slips from your bank's website as evidence that the funds were deposited. This is important because if you are ever audited by the I.R.S., you may need these records to prove the income you received.

3. **Financial Statements** – You will want to keep copies of your most recent Income Statements, Balance Sheets, Statement of Cash Flows, and Statement of Owner's Equity. If you ever decide to sell your music business or bring in investors to help you grow your

business, they will not just take your word for how successful your business has been. They will ask to see your financials so that they can confirm the business income and expenses. If you do not have the proper paperwork, you may miss out on opportunities if and when they become available.

4. **Copies of checks received.** Keep records of the money you are paid. This is important because the I.R.S. may require that you prove the income you listed on your tax return.

5. **Cancelled checks.** These are checks that you have written to other people to pay bills that have already cleared or been deposited. Keep a copy of them for your records to prove that you have paid your vendors. Cancelled checks also prove that you paid for business expenses that you are deducting.

6. **Receipts from purchases.** Receipts prove that the funds you spent from your business account were used for legitimate tax-deductible business expenses. Keeping copies of receipts from business purchases allows you to be prepared in case the I.R.S. audits you and asks you to provide evidence of the money you spent for your business.

7. **Business credit card statements** (if you have any)

8. **Any invoices that you have submitted to vendors.** This shows payments that vendors owe you and allows you to keep track of money you should be receiving.

Business Records

1. **Business contracts.** Anytime you agree to hire someone (e.g., producer, attorney, manager, distributor, graphic designer) or you agree to perform a service for someone (e. g., artist, band, songwriter, etc.) you need a contract in writing. This ensures that both parties understand the terms (how much they will be paid, when the work is due, who owns the rights) and protects you if you ever need to sue them for not performing.

    For example, if you and your band members disagree on how you decided to divide profits before you report them on your tax return, having a signed copy of your music contract would legally protect you and help you argue your position based on what everyone initially agreed to in writing. You should always keep a copy of the contract signed by both parties but at the minimum signed by the other party.

2. **Corporate Kit.** This is a binder that contains all of the important legal documents for your business including:

- Articles of Incorporation / Organization
- Bylaws
- Operating Agreement / Partnership Agreement / Shareholder Agreement
- Meeting Minutes. You should have minutes that document votes for major business decisions or purchases)
- Stock Certificates

My law firm frequently sells Corporate Kits, which are custom binders that keep all of your important business documents in a safe place to help you remain in compliance with the law.

3. **Employment Information.** You will also want to keep the following information regarding any employees or independent contractors that you hire to work within your music business:

- Independent Contractor Agreements
- Employment Agreements
- Employee Files
- 1099-MISC from performances and work done

Tax Records

As a business owner, you will likely be responsible for paying income taxes on a federal level, self-employment taxes, payroll taxes (if you have employees), state income taxes (if your state collects them), and sales taxes based on each album or tangible item that you sell.

You will want to keep records of the taxes that you pay so that you do not get in trouble with the I.R.S. An easy rule to remember with tax records is to keep a copy of everything. If you file a tax return, save a copy of it for your records. If you write a letter to the I.R.S. or if they send you a letter, keep a copy of it. Having these important documents on hand will help you prove that you are in compliance with the law if you are ever audited or ever need to reference them. Here are a few specific records to keep:

- **Income tax returns.** Make sure you keep a copy of the old tax returns you have filed just in case you are ever audited by the I.R.S.
- **Sales Tax Certificates.** Your state may require that you post this in your office or home office. Keep copies of the returns you submit and the sales tax you pay.
- **Letters & Correspondence from the I.R.S.** – If you ever send or receive a letter from the I.R.S., make sure you keep a copy in your business records.

These are just a few of the records you will want to keep as a business owner. Now that we understand recordkeeping, let's talk about the specific forms that you will need to file in order to pay your business taxes and stay in compliance with the law.

Chapter 13: Filing Business Taxes

An important part of being a business owner is making sure that you are paying your taxes. Although you can hire someone to handle it for you, it's always good to at least understand the basics of what you will be responsible for filing so that you can make sure that you are in good standing with the I.R.S.

Here are some of the main forms that you should expect to file for your music business depending on the type of business entity that you have chosen. My first book, *Start Your Music Business*, goes into detail regarding the different types of businesses and the advantages and disadvantages of each.

Also, keep in mind that every business owner's individual situation is different. I am not an accountant or CPA so you will need to check with your own accountant or tax specialist to make sure that these specific forms apply to your individual situation. The purpose of this chapter is to give you a point of reference regarding potential questions to ask and potential forms you can expect to complete depending on your business. Let's jump right in!

Taxes for Sole Proprietors

A sole proprietorship is a business owned by only one person so only the owner can file taxes for the business. If your music business is a sole proprietorship, you will likely need to complete the following:

1. **Income Tax Form 1040.** This is the basic form that is used to report your income and losses. You'll usually file this form along with other forms (schedules) based on your other sources of income (business, royalties, etc.) and your individual financial situation.

2. **Schedule C.** As a sole proprietor, you'll likely use this form to report the business income (money you made) or business losses of your music company. *If you have income from rents or royalties, you will likely use Schedule E.*

3. **Schedule SE Self-Employment Tax.** Since you work for yourself, you most likely have to pay self-employment taxes if you made $400 dollars or more after expenses (or meet other requirements). This form helps the government calculate how much you need to pay in taxes toward Social Security or Medicare

benefits since you are working for yourself and did not have an employer to take these amounts out of your check for you.

4. **1040 ES Estimated Taxes for Individuals.** Generally, you will be responsible for paying estimated tax payments or advance payments to the government before regular taxes are due if you think that you will owe at least $1,000 to the I.R.S. for the next year. Don't overlook this as estimated taxes allow you to contribute toward your upcoming taxes over time – instead of being hit by a big tax bill all at once in April.

Taxes for Partnerships

If your music business is a Partnership, you will likely be responsible for completing the following:

1. **Form 1065 Partnership Return of Income.** Use this form to report the money that your music company made or any business losses. A partnership itself does not pay taxes. Instead, this form is used to tell the IRS the amount of taxes each individual partner is responsible for paying.

2. **Schedule K-1.** Your music business is responsible for generating this I.R.S. form and giving it to each partner. This form will let each partner know how much income or business loss they need to include on their Schedule E when they will file with the IRS.

3. **Schedule E Supplemental Income and Loss.** Use this form to report the business income or business losses of your music company. Remember that you will have to pay taxes on all of the profit that the business made. This means that even if the business chose to leave some of the money in the business bank account and did not pay it out to the partners, you will still pay taxes on this profit.

4. **Schedule SE Self Employment Tax.** You're required to pay self-employment taxes if you made $400 dollars or more after expenses (net income). This form allows the government to calculate how much you need to pay in taxes that toward your Social Security or Medicare benefits.

5. **Income Tax Form 1040 (same as above).** This is the basic form that is used to report your income and losses. You'll usually file this form along with other forms (schedules) based on your other sources of income (business, royalties, etc.) and your individual financial situation.

6. **1040 ES Estimated Taxes for Individuals.** Generally, you will be responsible for paying estimated tax payments or advance payments to the government before regular taxes are due if you think that you will owe at least $1,000 to the I.R.S. for the next year.

Taxes for Limited Liability Companies (LLC)

If your music company is a Limited Liability Company, you are responsible for completing the following:

1. **Schedule C.** Use this form to report the business income or business losses of your music company if your music business is owned by only one person. You can request to be taxed like a partnership instead. This means you would file a Form 1065 and give a K-1 to the other Members (owners) of the LLC. See the partnership tax discussion above. *If you have income from rents or royalties, you will use Schedule E.*

2. **Schedule SE Self Employment Tax.** You are required to pay self-employment taxes if you made $400 dollars or more after expenses (or meet other requirements). This form allows the government to calculate how much you need to pay in taxes that will be used to contribute to your Social Security or Medicare benefits since you are working for yourself and did not have an employer to take these amounts out of your check for you.

3. **Income Tax Form 1040.** This is the basic form that is used to report your income and losses. You'll usually file this form along with other forms (schedules) based on your other sources of income (business, royalties, etc.) and your individual financial situation.

4. **1040 ES Estimated Taxes for Individuals.** Generally, you will be responsible for paying estimated tax payments or advance payments to the government before regular taxes are due if you think that you will owe at least $1,000 to the I.R.S. for the next year.

Taxes for Corporations

If your music company is a corporation you are responsible for completing the following:

1. **1120 US Corporation Income Tax Form.** Use this form if you are a "C Corporation."

2. **1120S US Estimated Tax for Corporations.** Use this form if you are a "S Corporation."

3. **Schedule K-1.** Your music company is responsible for generating this I.R.S. form and giving it to each shareholder. This form will let each partner know how much income or business loss that they need to include on their Schedule E when they will file with the IRS.

4. **Income Tax Form 1040.** This is the basic form that is used to report your income and losses. You'll usually file this form along with other forms (schedules) based on your other sources of

income (business, royalties, etc.) and your individual financial situation.

Make sure you visit www.IRS.gov for more specific tax requirements and speak with your accountant or tax specialist to ensure that you are in full compliance with the law.

Now that you have a basic understanding of taxes and how it all works, let's talk about a few team members that you may need to help you run your music business.

Chapter 14: Building Your Team

When you listen to interviews featuring successful people in the music industry, you're often left with the impression that they are just extraordinary people that were born with extraordinary talent and were able to climb to the top all by themselves. Although they're often very talented, most successful people in the music industry have a team behind them that contributes to their success.

For example, many of the most notable singers have worked tirelessly with vocal coaches and instructors to develop their singing, studied with dance instructors, worked with the best agents to book their shows, and the best publicity firms to manage their public image. They have lawyers structuring their deals, accountants making sure they keep more of their money and only pay the required amount in taxes, image consultants to make sure they are wearing the latest fashion, and managers to handle the day-to-day business operations of their music business. They are rarely doing it alone – but with the support of other extraordinarily talented people that help make them look good.

The same thing applies to you. You may not be a multi-platinum recording artist – but you still need to start building a team. You can try to navigate all of the various aspects of building a music business yourself – finances, publishing, booking, marketing, operations, legal, etc. If you do, you may risk burning out or quite simply spending so much time trying to familiarize yourself with all of the various disciplines that you don't have enough time to do what you do best – focus on your music.

Modern technology allows us to handle more things ourselves. However, there is always a cost to doing things yourself – time. We are each only given a limited number of hours in the day. The most successful people use their hours doing what they do best. They then build a team of people to help them in the other areas. This allows you to get more done since you are doing what you are good at instead of trying to become an expert at everything. It will also help you grow because you will be taking advantage of the experience of other professionals to move your business forward in all of the other areas.

There are lots of music books that will spend time discussing how to find a good manager, agent, and publisher to join your team. I'm going to spend a few moments discussing a few team members that are vitally important to your music business but are often overlooked by music business owners that are just getting started.

Why You Need an Attorney

While you are growing your music business, it may be tempting to skip the step of finding an attorney. You may have heard that attorneys are expensive. This fact alone can be discouraging. Perhaps, you may have had a bad experience with an attorney or you feel like you don't need one since you don't exactly know how an attorney could benefit your music business. Here are the top reasons you could benefit from having an attorney on your team:

1. **Contract Review**. A lawyer will review your contracts to make sure they say what you think they say. I know you may be thinking this is a waste of money – but it's not (this is why almost all of the most successful people in business and the music industry have their own attorney). Contracts are often written in "Legalese." This means the words may have different meanings in the law than what you would commonly think they mean. This is sometimes designed to make sure that one party (usually the person who had the contract made) can benefit over the other party without them knowing it.

The way that you can protect yourself is by making sure you have your *own* lawyer will read your contracts and tell you what they mean. Otherwise, you'll still be legally responsible for fulfilling the contract or facing the penalties of breaching (violating) the agreement once you sign the deal.

True story, I have had several clients that have shown me music contracts they were planning on signing and told me what they "thought" the contracts said. These were all very intelligent, educated, and successful people. One contract said that my client would be giving away all of the rights to his music (when he thought he was just licensing or giving them permission to use the songs for a limited period of time). One contract said my client would lose the rights to all of the music he had ever written (and would not be paid for this). Another contract said that my client would agree that virtually all touring and merchandise income would go to the label (even though my client was told he would get to keep 100% of the income). And the list goes on! The point is have your own lawyer review your contracts before you sign them!

2. **Structuring Deals.** A lawyer should analyze your contracts, offers, and business deals strategically to tell you what is in your best interests. This book does not cover everything. You need an attorney to review your specific opportunity to make sure that there are not additional terms included in the contract that were

not covered in this book. Again, I only highlighted a few key terms but there are tons of clauses that can be included in contracts and each agreement is different. The difference between a good deal and a bad deal is found in the terms and an experienced lawyer can help you make sure you have the best terms.

3. **Negotiations.** Once you know what the terms are, your lawyer will negotiate for you so that you do not jeopardize your industry relationships. Let your lawyer be the bad guy (or girl) – not you. Remember, lawyers are governed by strict rules that require them to fight for the best interests of their client. Even if you speak to the record label's attorney, they are biased because they are required by law to fight for the best interests of their client – which is the record label – not you. If you have your own lawyer, your lawyer can ask for more money, higher royalty splits, and argue for you to keep the rights to your music without you appearing to be ungrateful or difficult to work with. You can blame the negotiations on your lawyer while reaping the benefits of having contracts that pay you more and protect your legal interests.

4. **Structuring Your Empire** – In addition to contracts and negotiations, your lawyer can help you do the following:

    - Own your artist/band name and logo by obtaining a federal trademark;

- Make sure your assets (bank accounts, property, etc.) are protected in the event that you are sued;
- Help you raise capital (funds) from investors or business partners to grow your business;
- Help you hire staff and employees as well as buy or lease office space;
- Help you sell your business when you're ready;
- Defend your brand if someone is using your name or logo online without your permission;
- Establish a charity or foundation to allow you to give back to the community;
- Structure your business to take advantage of tax savings and protection from liability.

5. **Tax Savings.** You can typically deduct the legal fees you spend from your taxes as a business expense.

6. **Save money.** It's usually cheaper to have something reviewed than it is to fight in court. You will likely only spend a few hundred dollars having your agreement reviewed or having a legal consultation. However, most lawsuits start in the thousand dollar range.

How to afford an attorney

1. **Free consultations.** Many lawyers and law firms will offer a free consultation in which they will listen to your situation and outline

the steps they would take as well as give you a quote for their legal services. Take advantage of this opportunity to learn more about the attorney, their areas of specialization, and see if their fees are affordable.

2. **Flat fees.** Ask the attorney if they are willing to charge a flat fee (one-time fee) to review or draft your contract or to meet with you instead of billing you by the hour (which can end up being far more expensive).

3. **Maximize your time.** Make sure you have your specific questions written down in advance before you meet or call your attorney so that you can take advantage of the time you have with them. Some lawyers will even let you e-mail your questions in advance.

4. **Budget.** A legal consultation can cost you anywhere from $150-$400 depending on the attorney and their credentials. Put some money aside so that you can afford a session before you make major decisions regarding your music business.

What to look for in a good lawyer

Everyone has a different opinion as far as what qualities a good lawyer should have. Here are just a few of my thoughts on the subject:

1. **Experience.** Make sure they have represented people in the music industry before and have experience negotiating and dealing with the types of contracts and agreements that you need.

2. **Easy to talk to.** If you feel uncomfortable, intimidated or as if the lawyer does not have time for you then this may not be the attorney for you. Your lawyer should speak using words that you can understand and should be easy to talk to.

3. **Willing to answer questions.** If your attorney seems offended by you asking questions, then they may not be the best person. Make sure they are open and willing to give you both sides of the situation as well as answer your questions to make sure you understand everything that is taking place.

4. **Up front pricing.** A good lawyer should have enough experience to be able to estimate with reasonable certainty how much various services will cost you.

5. **Responsive.** Make sure the firm takes the time to get back to you in a timely manner before you hire them – or else you may never be able to reach them after you've paid them. I can't tell you how many of my firm's clients choose us because they were calling other firms and their calls were never returned.

6. **Reputation.** It's also helpful if the lawyer has positive reviews from past clients that they have represented in the past.

How to find a good lawyer

The best way to find a good lawyer is to get a referral from someone that has a good one. You can ask some of your friends in the music industry if they can refer you to a good attorney.

However, if this is unsuccessful, you can always go online and search for "entertainment lawyer in Chicago (insert your city)." You'll see more results than you can handle. Take your time and go through them. Try and get a feel for the different lawyers and call a few until you find one that you feel comfortable with.

Why you need an Accountant

I've worked for myself for a very long time and I still remember the first accountant that I hired. I was a law student and I had recently started my first business with a goal of graduating from law school debt free (which thank God worked out). At the time, I needed someone that knew how to do business taxes so I hired my first accountant. He ran a small office, had a friendly staff, and was able to make sure the taxes for my new LLC were filed correctly and on time.

As I started more businesses and began to invest in real estate, I realized that I needed a more intentional and sophisticated accounting system. The amount of taxes I was paying as a self-employed person was out of control. I knew my basic system of bookkeeping had to change. I also needed a new accountant. I needed someone that had experience handling financials for mid-large companies that could help my business setup a system that could accommodate our growth.

The first thing I did was make a list of the things that I needed help with:

- Selecting the right accounting software for my business;
- Setting up the accounting software to accurately record my financial transactions so that I could generate professional financial reports;
- Understanding how to read financial reports in order to know the health of my businesses;
- Making sure I was taking advantage of all of the available business deductions;
- Preparing my personal and business taxes with an emphasis on reducing my tax liability;
- Restructuring my business altogether to reduce my tax liability;
- Helping me setup payroll (system to pay full-time employees);

How to find a good accountant

Once I knew what I needed, it was time to find a new accountant. I asked for referrals from colleagues, searched online, and interviewed several accountants. Here were the things I was looking for:

- **CPA** – I wanted the accountant to be a Certified Public Accountant because I wanted them to have expertise instead of just having a bachelor's degree in accounting. The CPA I ended up hiring is actually getting a Masters degree in Taxation which is even better!

- **Experience** – I wanted the accountant to have worked previously for a large accounting firm so that they would have experience handling financials for mid-large companies and could handle the growth of my business. My CPA actually worked for an international firm and has worked for large companies in various industries.

- **Business owner** – I wanted the accountant to own the accounting firm. I was hoping this would mean the fees would be more reasonable. Plus, they would understand the role of a business owner and would appreciate my need for accounting solutions that would not take up all of my time.

- **Customer Service** – I also wanted to make that they answered the phone and returned calls and emails promptly

When you are just getting started, you may want to start by signing up for an online service or app that will let you manage or track your money yourself. Most of these services will allow you to keep track of clients that hire you, print invoices (for money they owe you), receipts (for money they have paid), track inventory, and view graphs and charts that show you how much money you are making and how much you are spending. Here are a few popular accounting software services:

http://quicken.intuit.com/
http://quickbooks.intuit.com/
http://na.sage.com

You will save lots of money in tax deductions by being organized and able to have good records to show what you actually spent. You can usually download your bank transactions directly into the app or program and it will categorize your expenses and help you generate financial reports.

As you grow, you may want to hire a part-time bookkeeper to manage the entries into your financial system. They will keep track of receipts, invoices and purchases and input these transactions into your accounting system. You can find a bookkeeper online or hire an online company such as Bench (www.Bench.co) to maintain your books (financial records).

Lastly, as your business continues to grow, you'll need to hire a CPA (and possibly a CFO) to provide you with strategic guidance for financially growing your business. Your CPA can provide tax advice, advice regarding major purchases and how they will affect your tax liability, and navigate you through the process of hiring your first employees and setting up payroll. Hiring a CPA is an expense that pays for itself.

In sum, there are a number of other team members that you will likely want to add to your team. However, making sure you find a good lawyer and a good accountant are just two professionals that are very important but are often overlooked.

Now that we have talked about the team that you will need in order to reach your goals, let's wrap up our journey together by talking about the benefits of giving back and how helping others can help you!

Chapter 15: Give Back

HOW GIVING BACK BENEFITS YOU

When we think of giving to other people, we sometimes think that we are the ones losing. We may feel that if we spend time doing something for someone else, we will have less time to advance our own goals. We may think that spending money on someone else will stop us from having resources to accomplish our own goals and dreams. We may also be reluctant to give or donate because we are not sure how our donation will be managed or used. Or we may simply want to hold onto the things that we have for fear that others will not appreciate what we have given them, will gain an unfair advantage over us, or fear that we will somehow lose out on a memory or the meaning behind something we have if we give it away.

I believe that giving to others will benefit you in more ways than it will even benefit the people you are helping. Here are just a few ways that giving back benefits you:

1. **Helps You Stay Positive** – When you serve food to the homeless, donate clothes to people that do not have anything to wear, or perform at an event that raises money to find a cure for people dying of an incurable disease, it makes it much easier for you to remain positive and thankful when you do not sell as many CDs as you hoped or when a concert you were looking forward to cancels. This is because giving back to others helps you keep things in perspective and know that there is always someone worse off than you. Instead of complaining about your hardships, you will think of the dire situation the people you helped are in and will instead be thankful that your loss or disappointment could have been far worse.

2. **Motivates You to Keep Going** – When you know your efforts are working toward a greater good, it inspires you to keep going because you know people are depending on you. The success of your band no longer means a new car and nice clothes that you may never wear. Instead, when you know that you have committed to giving away a portion of the proceeds to a good cause, your success means improving a local school, building low-income housing for the needy, providing college scholarships, or any other charitable act. I'm always encouraged by book sales because I use a portion of the proceeds to support deserving charities that are making a difference. You can do the same.

3. **Helps You Handle Failure** – When things do not work out for you, if you have been giving back to others, you won't take it personally as often but will know that things could always be worse and that failure is just a part of the road to success.

4. **Helps You Handle Stress** – Helping others helps you get your mind off of life's disappointments. If you find yourself feeling depressed, try taking the focus off of you by focusing on meeting someone else's needs. You may find that you will have a better perspective since you are reminded that there are people dealing with far more severe situations than you and that your situation may not be as bad as you thought.

5. **Attracts Good Things to Your Life** – I have found that the more generous I am with time (mentoring, helping, and investing in others) and my money (donating to support good causes), the more I find that people unexpectedly offer to help me or invest in my endeavors without me even having to ask. Never expect the people that you help to reciprocate. Instead, just know that God will bless you in other ways by your generosity toward the less fortunate.

6. **Helps You Enjoy Your Successes** – Success can be an unending quest. We can become so consumed by it that instead of even seeing the success we currently have, we are in constant pursuit for more. This causes us to be more critical and always want more as

opposed to seeing what we already have and being thankful. Spending your time focusing on the needs of others will help you see success in any accomplishment, big or small, and really appreciate your journey.

Ways to Give Back

Another obstacle that sometimes keeps us from giving to others is that we may think that we have to be a millionaire before we can afford to give things away. We envision the people that make donations as being successful philanthropists that are able to give large donations to build schools and fund major research projects. We feel that unless we have a lot to give, our small contributions are not worth giving. However, there are many ways that you can start giving back today:

1. **Speak to Students** – You can sign up as a volunteer at a nearby school and share your story to inspire students to make positive decisions. Remember, you only have to be one step ahead of a person to encourage them.

2. **Volunteer** – Think of a cause that you are passionate about (e.g., feeding the homeless, mentoring children, supporting cancer research, helping students afford a college education, etc.) Look up charities online that focus on the areas that you care about. Contact them and ask if they have any volunteer opportunities. Remember to follow-up. Many non-profits are run by volunteers

with small staff and may need you to remain persistent. Do not take it personally but allow your passion to keep you committed.

3. **Be a Mentor** – You don't have to be a celebrity to be a role model or hero to a child. There are students in need of after school mentors that will encourage them to stay in school, make positive decisions, and keep following their dreams. Contact local schools and community centers to find out how you can get involved.

4. **Donate Money** – You can agree to give a portion of all of your record sales to your favorite cause. You can also donate a percentage of everything you make to a local church or charity. I personally believe in tithing (giving 10% to a church that makes a difference in the community) as well as giving to local non-profits. This is something I've done this for years. It's sometimes helpful to share the charities or nonprofits that you are supporting with your fans and encourage them to join you in your efforts to give back. This will multiply the impact that you are making in the community. My law firm also donates to various charities throughout the year. Sometimes we share our charitable efforts with clients and supporters to encourage them to join in. Oftentimes we give and never even publicize it.

5. **Donate Merchandise & CDs** - You can sign up to donate albums and merchandise to a local children's hospital to brighten a child's day, a nursing home, or provide them to military troops overseas.

6. **Perform for Free** – You can contact a school, church, community center, hospital, nursing home, hospice, retirement community and volunteer to perform for free during the holidays.

7. **Donate Your Equipment** – Instead of selling your used music equipment online, you can choose to give away your old equipment each time you purchase a new piece of equipment to someone else in need. You can also sell the equipment and use the proceeds from the sale toward supporting a local charity.

8. **Be a Resource** - Share information you have learned with others that are trying to get where you are. You will find that it will come back to you and you will go farther than if you kept all of your information to yourself.

9. **Start Your Own Community Campaign** – My husband and I decided early in our marriage that we wanted to start a charitable tradition for our family. We collected clothing and purchased new toys and books and launched our annual "Clothing & Toy Drive for the Homeless." Each year, we contact our friends and family and encourage them to meet us at a local homeless shelter around the holidays to make a difference. Again, you don't have to be a

billionaire to mobilize your friends and network to do something to make a difference.

10. **Start Your Own Non-Profit** – As a college student, I started a non-profit to help teach high school students leadership, entrepreneurship, financial management and self-esteem principles. I didn't have all of the answers myself - but I knew that I was willing to share the information that I had acquired to benefit others. Since then, Revolution Leadership®, Inc. (www.RevolutionLeadership.org) is a 501(c)(3) tax-exempt non-profit that has served thousands of students and awards annual college scholarships. It is my passion and I do it for free because I love making a difference in the lives of young people.

It doesn't take much for you to do the same. Most people don't give back because they don't know where to get started. My law firm completes all of the legal paperwork for clients starting non-profits, answers their questions, and provides them with referrals to grantwriters and other service providers to secure the funding they need to fulfill their dream of helping others. Let us know if we can help.

11. **Invest in Family** – Although your music career may be important, take the time to build a relationship with your family (parents, siblings, spouse, and children). Schedule time each week to do something they enjoy. Ask them questions. Listen to their

interests. Find ways to support what they are doing. Be involved in their life. Speak kind and encouraging words to them. Inspire them to reach their goals. This will make more of an impact than selling all of the albums in the world.

Encourage Others to Give Back

Lastly, now that you are giving to others, encourage those around you to do the same. When you inspire others to give back, it increases the impact you are making. For example, if you begin collecting canned food to donate to a local Homeless Shelter to feed people in need, you may be successful at providing food for a few families. However, if you post a video on your artist website sharing with your fans that you are committed to supporting the local Homeless Shelter in your area and encouraging them to also donate, you are now impacting hundreds if not thousands of families.

Share openly with your supporters the causes that you believe in and the things you value. This will allow them to connect with you not only as an artist, band, songwriter or producer, but to know that by supporting you, they are supporting something greater that will have a lasting impact on society and the world. You will find that you will attract people that will enthusiastically support your efforts because they believe in the difference you are making.

If everyone used their gifts and talents to encourage one other person to make a difference, the world would be a better place. By investing this book, you have done just that because a portion of all proceeds are being donated to 501(c)(3) charitable non-profit organizations to support education and entrepreneurship.

Congratulations! We have now completed the "Run Your Music Business™" journey. Hopefully, you now have a better understanding of how to license your music to maximize your song related income, how to properly setup your own publishing company, and how to strategically grow your music catalog. We also discussed how to negotiate producer agreements, songwriter agreements, and recording artist agreements to make sure you're not cheated. By now, you should have a full arsenal of ways to work full-time in music for yourself and increase your music related revenue. Lastly, we explained how to properly manage your money to strategically position your business for growth, how to pay business taxes, and the benefits of giving back.

Final Words from the Author

If you enjoyed this book, please consider:

1. **Leave a review.** This helps the book gain more visibility online to help other people.
2. **Buy the first book** in my Music Law Series™ entitled "Start Your Music Business" (www.StartYourMusicBusiness.com)
3. **Tell a friend** (You can also recommend and add the book to your Amazon.com Wish List which helps us reach more people).
4. **E-mail me** your feedback or questions (Audrey@RunYourMusicBusiness.com)
5. **Visit our website** for more information, free legal tips, and more! (www.RunYourMusicBusiness.com)
6. **Follow me** on Twitter for free legal tips, special promotions and more. Over 11,000 followers and counting! (@AttorneyAudrey)
7. **Like our** Facebook page for free legal tips and updates that may not have made it into the book (Facebook.com/ChisholmLawFirm)
8. **Book me** to speak at your next music conference, seminar, workshop, concert or event (www.AudreyChisholm.com)

About the Author

Audrey K. Chisholm, Esq. is the founder and senior partner of Chisholm Law Firm, LLC. She is a nationally renowned attorney and represents individuals in the music business in entertainment, corporate, litigation, and intellectual property (copyright and trademark) legal matters.

She is a member of the Florida Bar Association. Her clients include Fortune 500 companies, record labels, songwriters, music publishers, producers and artists whose works have been featured on MTV®, American Idol®, and more. She is a sought after speaker at conferences and events and has spoken to audiences of over 13,000 people.

She is the published bestselling author of *"Start Your Music Business*™" and *"Run Your Music Business*™." Attorney Chisholm is also the founder of a federally recognized 501(c)(3) tax-exempt non-profit organization, Revolution Leadership®, Inc., that provides educational leadership programming, financial management, and entrepreneurship training, and awards college scholarships to high school students and has served thousands of students nationwide. She resides in Orlando, Florida with her husband, financial author Dr. Juan Chisholm and her daughter.

For more information, or booking, please visit:

www.AudreyChisholm.com

Twitter: @AttorneyAudrey

Facebook.com/ChisholmLawFirm

For more books and services, please visit:

www.StartYourMusicBusiness.com
www.RunYourMusicBusiness.com
www.ChisholmFirm.com
www.PurposeProperties.org
www.RevolutionLeadership.org